The Gospel of Mark

PROCLAIMING THE NEW TESTAMENT

The Gospel
of Mark

by

Ralph Earle

BAKER BOOK HOUSE
Grand Rapids 6, Michigan
1961

Library of Congress Catalog Card Number: 61-11088

PHOTOLITHOPRINTED BY CUSHING - MALLOY, INC.
ANN ARBOR, MICHIGAN, UNITED STATES OF AMERICA
1961

Dedicated
to
My faithful partner in proclaiming
the New Testament
with
all my sincere gratitude for her
love and patience

Editor's Foreword

In the series, Proclaiming the New Testament, an attempt is made to provide homiletical comments and ideas. The busy pastor needs to spend time in meditation if he is to offer the bread of life to his people. One of the best known methods of Bible study is to work through one book of the Bible at a time. This gives depth as well as breadth. It provides for the preaching of the whole counsel of God and not just a part of that revelation. As truth must reach people in various stages of growth and at different levels of reception, so there must be variety of communication.

The intention of this series is to stimulate men in the ministry to more definite study. Believing that the first rule of homiletics is to read and study the actual text of Scripture, this method brings ideas and suggestion. Here illustrations are limited as the individual should find his own as he reads or mingles with people, and as he is open to all the winds of God. No pastor can lead his people to a level of thought and spiritual experience higher than the one he occupies. God will not honor lazy men or men who imagine the Holy Spirit should prompt alone. God has given us a mind to use, a heart to love, a spirit to pray, and a will to study.

These results are possible from this approach. *One,* the pastor and student will find suggestive ideas. As Charles H. Spurgeon said of William Gurnall (1616-79), a Puritan, "I have found his work the best thought-breeder in all our library. I should think more discourses have been suggested by it than by any other. I have often resorted to it when my own fire has been burning low...." *Two,* the user will see how to study an entire book of the Bible for preaching values. *Three,* the man of God will be encouraged to begin the study of the Bible book for himself and find by this method other treasures of homiletical insight.

While using the King James or Authorized Version, the student should compare with all other versions and translations as well as the original text when available.

Many and varied are the commentaries available for the profit of the preacher. These include the following:

I. *Critical.* This deals with the text in the light of biblical criticism, seeking to apply historical principles and a rational approach to the text, e.g., *The International Critical Commentary, The Moffatt New Testament Commentary, The Expositor's Greek Testament,* and the commentaries of H. A. W. Meyer, and Keil and Delitsch.

II. *Exegetical.* This seeks to lead out the exact meaning of the text in terms of the words and idioms in the light of their background and use originally, e.g., *The Westminster Commentaries, The New International Commentary on the New Testament, The Evangelical Commentary on the New Testament,* and the commentaries of R. C. H. Lenski, J. P. Lange, and W. Hendriksen.

III. *Expository.* This expounds and applies the dominant theme of each section or unit in the light of history and with relevance to the present, e.g., *The Expositor's Bible, The Interpreter's Bible, Calvin's Commentaries, The Pulpit Commentary,* and *An American Commentary on the New Testament.*

IV. *Devotional.* This brings out the inner sense or the spiritual essence as applied to the soul in meditation. Here is the stimulus to the spiritual life of the believer, e.g., *A Devotional Commentary,* and Matthew Henry's *Commentary on the Whole Bible.*

The present type of book is neither a Bible study book nor a book of outlines. It is not a commentary as the above. We seek to encourage the preacher to engage in the reading and studying of the book to find the homiletical units. As "the servant of the Word" let him work toward this ideal:

the Historical setting,
the Expository meaning,
the Doctrinal value,
the Practical aim,
the Homiletical form

The First Presbyterian Church
of Seattle, Washington

Ralph G. Turnbull
General Editor

Author's Introduction

According to ancient tradition the Gospel of Mark reflects the preaching of Peter. He was the man who had three thousand converts at the close of his first sermon. We can afford to listen to him today.

There is a freshness about this Gospel that inspires good homiletics. Here we find rapid action, vivid detail, picturesque language. Many a preacher might be jolted out of his rut — another name for long grave — by letting the impact of Mark really hit him.

It is hoped that the present volume will be at least a lure to further study and finer preaching in the Gospel of Mark. The suggestions contained herein are just signposts, pointing the way to a richer, more rewarding ministry of the Word.

Ralph Earle

Contents

Mark	1.	The Gospel of Jesus Christ	11
Mark	1.	The Highest Calling	14
Mark	1.	The Price of Prayer	17
Mark	1.	Love's Willingness	20
Mark	2.	The Faith That Works	23
Mark	2.	Jesus and the Sabbath	26
Mark	3.	Success in Successors	30
Mark	4.	A Quartet of Human Hearts	33
Mark	4.	Little Is Much If God Is in It	37
Mark	4.	With the Master on Board	40
Mark	5.	Public Enemy No. 1	44
Mark	5.	Faith Receiving	47
Mark	5.	Faith That Knows No Failure	50
Mark	6.	A King's Uneasy Conscience	53
Mark	6.	The Reward of Obedience	56
Mark	6.	A Presence in the Darkness	59
Mark	7.	The Sin of Ceremonialism	62
Mark	7.	The Tenderness of the Master	65
Mark	8.	Jesus the Messiah	68
Mark	8.	The Pathway to Life	71
Mark	9.	The Transfigured Christ	74
Mark	9.	The High Cost of Carelessness	77
Mark	10.	Jesus on Divorce	80
Mark	10.	True Greatness	83
Mark	11.	The Triumphal Entry	86
Mark	11.	The Power of Faith	89
Mark	12.	Should We Pay Taxes?	92
Mark	12.	The Primacy of Love	95
Mark	13.	The Whole Gospel for the Whole World	98
Mark	13.	The Master's Return	101
Mark	14.	Gethsemane	104
Mark	14.	The Big Fisherman's Worst Hour	107
Mark	15.	Barabbas or Jesus?	110
Mark	15.	Saving Oneself or Saving Others	113
Mark	16.	The Message of the Empty Tomb	116

Mark 1

THE GOSPEL OF JESUS CHRIST

1:1. "The beginning of the gospel of Jesus Christ, the Son of God."

I. HISTORICAL SETTING. Mark was writing in Rome for Romans. He wished to present Jesus Christ as the Mighty Conqueror and at the same time as the Suffering Servant of Jehovah. So he omitted the genealogy of Jesus (found in Matthew and Luke), as well as the Infancy Narratives. Romans were interested in a man's deeds rather than his descent. Mark gives us little of the words of Jesus, but concentrates on His deeds and death.

II. EXPOSITORY MEANING. "Gospel" means "good news." It is not a proposition to be debated nor a doctrine to be defended. It is news to be proclaimed. "Of Jesus Christ" is objective genitive, not subjective. So the verse might be translated: "The beginning of the glad tidings about Jesus Christ, the Son of God." This first verse is probably the heading for the book of Mark, though some apply it only to the ministry of John the Baptist. "Jesus Christ" was accepted and used as a proper name by the time Mark wrote his Gospel. Originally it was "Jesus the Christ"; i e., the Messiah.

III. DOCTRINAL VALUE. Commonly *Mark* has been thought of as the historical Gospel, in greatest contrast to *John,* which is spiritual and theological. But increasingly it has been recognized in recent years that Mark's Gospel has a strong theological purpose. Mark, as well as John, is presenting Jesus as the Son of God. In line with this the tendency now is to accept the last phrase "son of God" as genuine, even though it is missing in some of the early Greek manuscripts. It is included in the Revised Standard Version (1952) and also

11

in the New English Bible (1961). It is defended by F. C. Grant in *The Interpreters Bible* (VII, 648).

IV. PRACTICAL AIM. Mark's primary purpose was to introduce men to Jesus Christ as Son of God and Savior. That is the first responsibility of every preacher. All men need a divine Savior.

V. HOMILETICAL FORM

Theme: "The Gospel of Jesus Christ."

Introduction: Long the world had waited. For dreary centuries sin had multiplied, with its consequent sorrow and suffering. Tear-stained eyes looked heavenward, sometimes it seemed in vain. But at last came the joyful proclamation: The Messiah, the Savior, has come!

A. *The Beginning of the Gospel*

Too often we have thought of the gospel as a creed, of the Bible as a textbook in systematic theology. But the Old Testament begins with history: the record of God's dealings with His chosen people. Also the New Testament begins with history: the account of Jesus' earthly life, death and resurrection, and the spread of the early church following Pentecost.

Likewise the gospel begins with history. It is preëminently "His Story." Mark describes this beginning of the gospel. He gives the story of the Conquering Christ and Suffering Servant who thereby became the Savior of mankind.

B. *The Gospel of Jesus Christ*

The noun *euangelion,* "gospel," is a favorite with Paul. He uses it sixty times in his epistles. In contrast it occurs only four times in Matthew's Gospel, eight times in Mark's, and not at all in Luke's or John's. But the verb *euangelizo,* "preach the gospel" is used by Luke ten times in his Gospel and fifteen times in *Acts.* The gospel is not a credal formula to be buried in a theological tome. It is glorious good news to be proclaimed. It is something to *evangelize.*

Apart from Jesus Christ there is no gospel. The so-called "social gospel" is a misnomer. Other religions began with a sage who promulgated a philosophy of life. Christianity began with a divine Savior. It is more than a creed or an ethic. Christianity is Christ. That is the gospel.

C. *The Son of God*

The deity of Jesus is the foundation of the gospel. Unless the Son of God had come to earth there would be no good news to proclaim. It is a striking fact that no other great world religion claims that its founder was divine. Moses, Confucius, Gautama, Laotze, Mohammed — all were mere men. Jesus Christ is the eternal Son of God. Therein lies the utter uniqueness of Christianity. It alone is a true religion of salvation, because it alone has an adequate Savior.

To deny the deity of Jesus Christ is to remove the foundation of our religion. No building can stand when its foundation is gone. Christianity without a divine Christ is no longer Christianity. And it is certainly no gospel.

Mark 1

THE HIGHEST CALLING

1:17. "And Jesus said unto them, Come ye after me, and I will make you to become fishers of men."

I. HISTORICAL SETTING. After His public inauguration (the Baptism) and His private initiation (the Temptation) — both of which took place in the southern part of Palestine — Jesus went north to Galilee. Here He made Capernaum the headquarters of His great Galilean ministry. Walking along the lakeshore nearby He saw four fishermen and called them to follow Him.

II. EXPOSITORY MEANING. "Come ye after me" means "Be my disciples." The rabbis of that day had disciples who "came after them." So these four fishermen were to go to school to Jesus, that He might teach them how to become fishers of men.

III. DOCTRINAL VALUE. Jesus is shown here as the Master of men. He said, "Come," and men forsook all to follow Him. He still speaks with divine authority, and people are still hearing and heeding His call.

IV. PRACTICAL AIM. To challenge each Christian to a life of consecrated stewardship. All of us should be fishers of men. Only by following Christ can we learn the secrets of successful soul-winning.

V. HOMILETICAL FORM
Theme: "The Highest Calling."
Introduction: The highest calling is that of being a soul-winner. This surpasses the most exalted political position, the supreme social recognition, even the special office of the ministry. There is no greater task on earth. And every Christian is called to this task.

A. *The Divine Call.* "Come ye after me."

Soul-winning is an art. It must be learned. Jesus is the master Teacher. He invites every Christian to follow Him, to sit at His feet, to learn of Him. It is at once our greatest privilege and responsibility.

This call is more than an invitation; it is a command. It is in the imperative mood. We have no choice. If we refuse to follow, we are disobeying the King. He calls; we must come.

"Come ye after me" means "Come, follow me." One cannot be a Christian and choose his own path. He must follow Christ.

For these four fishermen, following Christ meant forsaking everything for full time service. While this is not literally true for every Christian, there is a very real sense in which everyone who would follow the Master must forsake all. There has to be a surrender of our will to His will. That is the price of discipleship.

B. *The Divine Concern.* "I will make you."

Two things this verse suggests. The first is that unless we follow Jesus we cannot become fishers of men. There is no way by which He can make us such except by His own example. There are some things in life which cannot be learned from books; they come only by personal contact. No amount of inspiration and instruction from human sources can take the place of fellowship with the supreme Soul-winner. Only as we catch His passion for souls, His spirit of compassionate love, can we become soul-winners. There are no short cuts to success in this field.

The second thing this verse suggests is that if we really follow Jesus we *shall* become fishers of men. We have His promise for it. If we are not winning souls to Christ, it is because somehow we are failing to follow. Fellowship with the Master will "make" us fishers of men. The challenge is ours.

C. *The Divine Commission.* "fishers of men."

Detailed assignments differ. One is called to the foreign field, another to labor at home. Some are designated as pastors, others are commissioned as evangelists. But all are called to win souls. This is the commission that comes to every Christian.

Successful fishing demands skill. That is also true of fishing for men. It is the most exacting work, but at the same time the most rewarding. It requires patience as well as knowledge. Nothing in life is more important. Christ is still calling His disciples to be fishers of men.

On the phrase "fishers of men" the sainted Bishop Ryle wrote: "It is the oldest name by which the ministerial office is described in the New Testament.... The minister who does not strive to live up to this name, has mistaken his calling."

Mark 1

THE PRICE OF PRAYER

1:35. "And in the morning, rising up a great while before day, he went out, and departed into a solitary place, and there prayed."

I. HISTORICAL SETTING. Jesus had just had an extremely busy day in Capernaum. At the synagogue service in the morning He not only taught the assembled crowd but also cast an unclean spirit out of a man. When He and His disciples returned to Peter's house for dinner they found that apostle's mother-in-law bedridden with a sudden, severe fever. Again the Master met the need. As soon as the Sabbath ended at sunset, so that burdens could be carried, multitudes thronged to Him, bringing those who were diseased and demon-possessed. Mark records Peter's observation that "all the city was gathered together at the door." Yet this healing service after sunset was followed by a prayer meeting before sunrise.

II. EXPOSITORY MEANING. Mark uses three adverbs to make more graphic and vivid the fact that Jesus rose very early to pray. The first means "early" or "in the morning." The second means "at night." The third means "very" or "exceedingly." Put together, the phrase indicates: "very early in the morning, while it was still night."

Likewise three verbs (one a participle) describe Jesus' action. All three are in the aorist tense, suggesting prompt, immediate movement. Literally the Greek reads: "having risen he went out and went away." He lost no time in getting to prayer.

"Solitary" is literally "desert" or "wilderness." It means primarily an uninhabited area. The idea here is of a lonely spot.

III. DOCTRINAL VALUE. If Jesus Christ the eternal Son of God needed fellowship with His Father, how much more do

we! The true humanity of Jesus is reflected in His prayer life.
Though filled with the Spirit, He needed to pray.

IV. PRACTICAL AIM. To show how utterly essential prayer
is to every Christian. Also the price of prayer: self-discipline.

V. HOMILETICAL FORM
  Theme: "The Price of Prayer."
  Introduction: Prayer is the breath of the soul. Paul ex-
horted: "Pray without ceasing." When we stop breathing we
die physically. When we stop praying we die spiritually. There
is no substitute for prayer. To the one who walks close to God
prayer is as natural as breathing.

  A. *The Priority of Prayer.* "And in the morning, rising up
a great while before day . . ."
  Jesus had had a very strenuous day. Probably the healing
service had lasted to a late hour. The Master had every excuse
for lying abed the next morning. He needed sleep.

  Instead He rose to pray. Not just any time, but "in the early
morning, long before daylight" (Moffatt). With Jesus prayer
had the highest priority.

  Almost all those who have prayed successfully have found
that the best time for prayer is early in the morning. There
are many reasons for this. One needs to pray before his mind
becomes cluttered with the many cares and duties of the day.
Usually the mind is clearer and fresher at an early hour. Not
least important is the quiet atmosphere that is essential to the
highest communion with God. It is much more difficult to pray
when one is caught up in the bustle and hustle of the distract-
ing daylight hours. If we would have the dew of heaven on our
hearts we must seek it early. In most lives prayer either comes
first or not at all — except perhaps for a meaningless perfunc-
tory performance at bedtime.

  B. *The Place of Prayer.* "he went out, and departed into a
solitary place."
  Next in importance to the time of prayer is the place of
prayer. Real "private devotions" require being alone with
God. Ideally this means isolation. If that cannot be found,
then extra insulation of heart and mind is needed.

In the modern home it is very difficult to find a lonely spot. One cannot hope to pray with radio or television blaring away. In some homes the only escape may be an early hour before others rise and turn on their radios. The earnest seeker after the sense of God's presence will be willing to pay the price of self-discipline to find the time and place for solitary communion with his Lord. Only those who do so at least in a measure really keep alive spiritually.

C. *The Practice of Prayer.* "and there prayed."

The only way to learn to pray is to pray. Reading books on prayer helps. But one can as quickly learn to ride a bicycle by reading about it as one can learn to pray thus. Perfection comes only through much practice.

It is possible to be in a solitary place at an early hour and yet fail to pray. The time and place are no guarantee against a wandering mind. Jesus really prayed. In this, as in all else, we are called to follow Him.

Mark 1

LOVE'S WILLINGNESS

1:40, 41. "If thou wilt, thou canst make me clean ... I will; be thou clean."

I. HISTORICAL SETTING. After His sunrise prayer meeting Jesus refused to return to Capernaum for another great healing service, though the crowds clamored for Him. Instead He announced that He must go to other towns to preach (lit. "proclaim"). It was for this reason He came forth from heaven (v. 38). So He made a tour of Galilee, preaching (proclaiming) in the synagogues and casting out demons (v. 41). Somewhere along the way a leper came to Him, asking to be cleansed.

II. EXPOSITORY MEANNG. "Came" (v. 40) is in the Greek "comes." Mark loves to use the historical present to add greater vividness to his narratives, to give it the sense of immediacy. A "leper" has always been looked upon as unclean. Scholars seem agreed that the leprosy of Bible times was a skin disease, which differed from the leprosy of today. But it made its victim ceremonially unclean. Luke the physician says the man was "full of leprosy" (5:12).

"Moved with compassion" is an aorist passive participle. To bring out the force of the aorist tense it might be better to translate it "gripped with compassion." This was Jesus' immediate reaction to human sorrow and suffering. The word "compassion" is from Latin, "sympathy" from Greek — words with exactly the same connotation. To have real compassion or sympathy we must suffer with sorrowing hearts. Jesus did.

"I will" is not the future tense of the word "to be." The Greek verb *thelo* means "will" or "wish," expressing an activity of the will. So the two phrases (vv. 40, 41) could be translated: "If you are willing . . . I am willing." "Be thou clean"

20

is the aorist passive imperative. It means: "Be thou (right here and now, immediately) cleansed."

III. DOCTRINAL VALUE. Again the deity of Jesus is emphasized. He was able to cure instantaneously the disease of leprosy. Also we have the beautiful, comforting truth that God's power is matched by God's love. When power is controlled by love, we are safe.

IV. PRACTICAL AIM. To show the willingness of Jesus to meet our every need, if we only ask Him. Whatever the nature of our need, He is always willing to help.

V. HOMILETICAL FORM

Theme: "Love's Willingness."

Introduction: The commonest concept of God is that He is the all-powerful, eternal Being who created the heavens and the earth. In this atomic age we are just beginning to realize something of the terrifyingly tremendous power that is built into the structure of our universe. The outstanding revelation of God in nature is that of His infinite power.

Yet nowhere in Scripture do we read, "God is power." Instead we find twice "God is love" (I John 4:8, 16). God has power. He displays His power. But His essential nature is *love*. That is the lesson taught by our text.

A. *The Man's Fear.* "If thou wilt."

Fear is always an evidence of lack of faith. How awful to say to Divine Love Incarnate, "If you are willing"! Love is always willing. The leper had seen Jesus' *power* demonstrated. But somehow he had failed to see His love disclosed. How little he understood the real Christ. Sadder still, how little we understand Him! Too often we doubt divine love. The disconcerting truth is that the reason we doubt divine love is that we do not know well enough the divine Lover. When we become sufficiently acquainted with some saints down here, we never question their willingness to do the thing that is right and kind and generous. Why should we doubt Christ's willingness to help us at the place of our deepest need?

B. *The Man's Faith.* "Thou canst make me clean."

About the Master's power the man had no question. "You

are able," he said. His faith in Jesus' ability was unwavering. He had seen the mighty Conqueror meet disease and demons, and defeat them both. What he had failed to sense was that Christ's healing ministry was as much an evidence of divine love as it was of supernatural power. It was power impelled and propelled by love. Power controlled by selfish hate is the most dangerous thing in the world. Power controlled by unselfish love is the greatest blessing mankind can know. In this day of discovery of the secrets of fission and fusion God grant that our world may learn that lesson before it is too late!

We cannot doubt God's power. Let us not be guilty of doubting His love.

C. *The Master's Fulfilment.* "I will; be thou clean."

Only two words in the original: *thelo, katharistheti.* It takes six in English to translate them: "I am willing; be thou cleansed."

The Master's response was immediate. No chiding the man's unbelief. No holding off his hesitating heart. No reproof for his half faith. What comfort in that word, "I am willing"! God forgive us for ever doubting divine love.

The Master fulfilled the man's faith. But He did more. He went the second mile and banished his lingering fear. Have you ever noticed how often in the Scriptures the Divine confronts the human with the words "Fear not"?

Not only did Jesus say to the anxious leper, "Be thou cleansed," but "as soon as he had spoken, immediately the leprosy departed from him, and he was cleansed" (v. 42). He spoke, and it was done. No word of God shall be without power. It was so in creation (Gen. 1:3, 6, 9, 11, 14, 20, 24, 26). It is still true today.

Mark 2

THE FAITH THAT WORKS

2:5. "When Jesus saw their faith, he saith unto the sick of the palsy, Son, thy sins be forgiven thee."

I. HISTORICAL SETTING. Jesus had spent some time evangelizing the villages of Galilee (1:39). As a Jewish rabbi He could go into any synagogue on the Sabbath Day and be invited to say whatever He wished. This custom of the day was of tremendous advantage to Christ, as it was later to Paul.

Finally Jesus returned to Capernaum, where He was making His headquarters. It was heard *(ekousthe)*, "He is at home." Immediately the great crowds thronged once more to Him to be healed. But true to His mission, "He was speaking to them the Word" (so the Greek).

II. EXPOSITORY MEANING. "One sick of the palsy" (v. 3) is one word in the Greek — *paralyticon.* Today we would say, "a paralytic." The term "press" (v. 4) has no reference to newspapers! It is simply the common Greek word *ochlos,* which means "crowd." "Uncovered" is literally "unroofed." "Bed" is "pallet," probably nothing more than a heavy quilt. It acted as a stretcher.

"Thy sins be forgiven thee" (v. 5) is a bad mistranslation. It sounds like an expressed wish — "may they be." The Greek, however, is an assertion. Manuscripts differ between the present and perfect tenses, but both in the indicative. The former would be, "Your sins are forgiven"; the latter, "Your sins have been forgiven." "Reasoning" (v. 6) is the verb *"dialogizomai."* It might be translated "debating" or "arguing." The "scribes" were those who studied and taught the Scriptures.

III. DOCTRINAL VALUE. Jesus demonstrated His deity not only in healing the paralytic instantly but also in forgiving his sins. The latter is a divine prerogative, as the scribes recognized. Since they did not accept Jesus as the Son of God they charged Him with blasphemy for claiming the authority to forgive sins. But Jesus made good His claim by healing the man.

IV. PRACTICAL AIM. To show that Jesus can forgive sins and also heal the paralysis of sin, freeing one to walk in the newness of life. But someone must work to get the sinner to the Savior.

V. HOMILETICAL FORM

Theme: "The Faith That Works."

Introduction: James wrote in his Epistle (2:18) : "Show me your faith apart from your works, and I by my works will show you my faith" (literal translation) .

"When Jesus saw their faith." How did He see it? By their works! They demonstrated their faith by bringing the paralytic to Jesus. They believed the Master could heal him. Faith produced action. The faith that works (succeeds) is the faith that *works*.

A. *The Setting.* "It was heard, 'He is at home.' "

Probably the paralytic had heard about the momentous day in Capernaum when Jesus had healed so many. It began with delivering the demoniac in the synagogue from his affliction (1:21-28) . Then came the healing of Peter's mother-in-law (1:29-31) , followed by the great sunset healing service (1:32-34) . Somehow the poor paralytic was left out. Perhaps no friends appeared to take him to Jesus.

We can imagine him saying to himself: "Well, I can wait until tomorrow. Then somebody will see that I reach the Healer." But the next day Jesus was gone! After an early prayer meeting he had gone elsewhere. The man's hopes were all dashed to the ground. Days of disappointment followed.

Then suddenly came the exciting news, "He is home again!" Four sympathetic friends came hurrying to the paralytic's side. Each grabbed a corner of the padded quilt and quickly they carried the helpless man to the Master.

B. *The Scene.* "When they could not come nigh . . . they uncovered the roof."

Eagerly the stretcher-bearers hurried to the house where Jesus was teaching. But already a crowd had gathered. The place was packed so tightly with people that it was impossible to reach Jesus. At least so it seemed.

But, "all things are possible to him that believeth." The four friends showed their faith by their works. Up an outside stairway they carried the paralytic to the flat roof of the one-story home. Vigorously they attacked the job of digging away the hard-packed dirt and tearing a wide hole in the branches laid on cross beams. Before the startled gaze of those who sat below they lowered the paralytic on his pallet right down in front of Jesus. They had succeeded. They had done their part. The rest was up to the Master.

We might call these four friends Prayer, Persistence, Patience, and Perseverance. Doubtless they encouraged each other in overcoming the apparently impossible obstacles in the way of getting the paralytic to Jesus. Together they did the job. What would happen today if four people would dedicate themselves unitedly to the task of winning one helpless sinner to Jesus?

C. *The Sequel.* "Thy sins be forgiven thee. . . . Arise, and take up thy bed."

The man's first need was forgiveness. His paralysis was a symbol of his sin. It may possibly have been due to a serious guilt complex. In any case, Jesus first forgave the man his sins.

The scribes were horrified. This was blasphemy. But Jesus proved He had authority to forgive sins by healing the man instantly.

The four friends gained more than they had planned for the paralytic. He was healed both physically and spiritually. What a celebration they must have had at his house that day.

Thousands around us are paralyzed by sin. They seem helpless to do anything about it. But prayer, persistence, patience, and perseverance can bring them effectively to the Great Physician.

Mark 2

JESUS AND THE SABBATH

2:28. "The Son of man is Lord also of the sabbath."

I. HISTORICAL SETTING. In the section 2:1—3:6 we find Jesus five times in conflict with the Pharisees. The first controversy was over His claim to forgive sins (2:1-12), the second because of His eating with publicans and sinners (2:13-17), the third about the matter of fasting (2:18-22), the fourth because the disciples plucked some heads of wheat on the Sabbath Day (2:23-28), and the fifth because he healed the man with a withered hand on the Sabbath (3:1-6). The last two may well be treated together, since they are concerned with the same subject — keeping the Sabbath.

II. EXPOSITORY MEANING. "Corn fields" (2:23) should be "grainfields" in an American translation. In England wheat is still called "corn." But to the American reader "corn" connotes something very different. So "ears of corn" should be "heads of grain." We cannot be sure whether this was barley harvested earlier and eaten by the poor people or wheat (ripe in May).

The mention of Abiathar the high priest (2:26) poses a little problem. The Old Testament account indicates that his father Ahimelech was high priest when this incident took place (I Sam. 21:1-8). The best solution is that "in the days of Abiathar the high priest" should be interpreted as meaning during the lifetime of Abiathar, who became the outstanding high priest of that period. "Shewbread" is better translated "bread of the Presence" (Hebrew). The Greek literally says, "loaves of the presentation." Fresh loaves of bread were placed before the Lord in the Holy Place each Sabbath (Lev. 24:5-9).

"Watched" (3:2) is a strong word in the Greek. Literally it means, "They kept watching him closely." Wycliff (first

English version of the Bible) translated it, "Thei aspieden Hym." That conveys the correct meaning. The Pharisees (Luke 6:7) were spying on Jesus, hoping to catch Him in a trap.

"When he had looked round about" (3:5) is all one word in the Greek, an aorist participle. On the other hand "being grieved" is a present participle, indicating continuing action or state. The momentary flash of anger was accompanied and followed by an abiding feeling of deep grief (an intensive compound is used in the Greek). That is the test of Christian anger. Is it like that of Christ? "Hardness" is better rendered "hardening." It indicates moral insensibility. A good English equivalent is "callousness." The Greek word was used for the formation of a hard substance on the bones. The Pharisees had become brittle in their rigid legalism.

III. DOCTRINAL VALUE. The sovereignty of the Son of Man is strongly asserted in the text. The compassion of Christ for human need is also highlighted in this passage (2:23 — 3:6).

IV. PRACTICAL AIM. To seek to understand Jesus' attitude toward the Sabbath as giving us guidance for Sabbath observance.

V. HOMILETICAL FORM
   Theme: "Jesus and the Sabbath."
   Introduction: Five times in little more than a chapter (2:1— 3:6) we find Jesus in conflict with the Pharisees. The last two times it had to do with keeping the Sabbath. Our present text lies between these two incidents (2:23-27 and 3:1-6) and ties them together. It gives us Jesus' conclusion of the matter.

   A. *The Controversy.* "Behold, why do they on the sabbath day that which is not lawful?"
   It was not a question of stealing. The Mosiac law specifically permitted the plucking of grain to eat from another's field (Deut. 23:25). The complaint was that in picking the heads of wheat, rubbing out the kernels in their hands, and blowing away the chaff the disciples were harvesting, thresh-

ing, and winnowing grain. This is a typical example of the
legalists' habit of making a mountain out of a mole hill. To
use Christ's own figure, the Pharisees were straining out a gnat
and swallowing a camel!

Jesus defended His disciples by calling attention to the
example of their hero king. David in an emergency had taken
the sacred bread of the Presence, which only the priests had a
right to eat. Actually, the rabbis struggled over this problem
and came to the conclusion that a man was justified in eating
the sacred loaves rather than starving. God's laws were given
that men might live, not die. With this Jesus agreed.

B. *The Conflict.* "They watched him . . . that they might
accuse him."

Jesus came into still sharper conflict with the Pharisees
over the question of healing on the sabbath day. Noting in the
synagogue a man with his hand all dried up (perfect passive
participle), they rightly judged that the compassionate Christ
might wish to heal him. So they watched Him narrowly.

Healing on the Sabbath Day came under the category of
forbidden labor. The rabbis drew fine distinctions in these
matters. It was permitted on the Sabbath to give medication
that might ease pain. But a poultice could not be placed on
a boil, for it would draw the pus and this would be work!
Actually, all that Jesus did was to speak to the man. When
he obeyed the Master's command to stretch out his hand, it
was healed.

The fury of the Pharisees is seen in that they, the religious
leaders, went out and plotted with the politicians (Herodians)
"how they might destroy him" (3:6). It was wrong for Jesus
to heal a man on the Sabbath, but it was perfectly all right
for them on that day to conspire to murder Him! What did
Jesus say about wanting to take a speck out of your brother's
eye when you have a log in your own?

C. *The Conclusion.* "The sabbath was made for man, and
not man for the sabbath."

Legalists are interested in precepts. God is interested in
persons. Legalists must protect their pet prejudices and private
opinons, no matter what the cost in human personality. What

matters if souls are offended and forever lost as long as we preserve intact our rigid regulations? Against this divine love reacted.

What is proper on the Sabbath or Lord's Day? God provided the Sabbath for man's welfare and highest good — physically, mentally, and spiritually. He who made us knows we need to rest and worship one day in seven. We flout His law to our own detriment.

On the Lord's Day we should do what we sincerely feel is pleasing to the Lord of the Sabbath. No honest heart will go far astray at this point. To please Christ is to be a Christian.

Mark 3

SUCCESS IN SUCCESSORS

3:14. "And he ordained twelve, that they should be with him, and that he might send them forth to preach."

I. HISTORICAL SETTING. Jesus had already called several disciples to follow Him. John 1:35-51 tells of the first five or six — six if John also brought his brother James. Mark has recorded the call to full time service that came to the four fishermen on the shores of Galilee (1:16-20), as well as to Levi (Matthew), the tax collector (2:14). But now something new takes place. Jesus selects twelve of His disciples to be apostles, His chosen messengers or missionaries. Appropriately this event took place on a mountain (v. 13).

II. EXPOSITORY MEANING. "Ordained" is better rendered "appointed." The former suggests an ecclesiastical ceremony which is probably not a correct picture. The Greek simply says "made." After "twelve" the two oldest manuscripts add: "whom also he named apostles." It would seem that twelve were chosen to represent the twelve tribes of Israel. "Canaanite" (v. 18) should be "Cananaean." Luke (6:15) interprets this as "the Zealot." This could mean simply that he was a very zealous individual, or it might indicate that he was a member of the party of Zealots who became prominent later.

III. DOCTRINAL VALUE. Again the sovereignty of Christ as Lord is emphasized. He summoned those He wished as His ambassadors, and they came to Him. The doctrine of divine healing is also suggested (v. 15).

IV. PRACTICAL AIM. To emphasize the importance of the ministry for the carrying on of the work of the kingdom.

V. HOMILETICAL FORM

Theme: "Success in Successors."

Introduction: A man's success is measured not so much by what he actually accomplishes in his own lifetime as by what provision he makes for posterity. Success cannot be properly gauged except in terms of the long view. Not a meteor-like flash across the sky but a permanent deposit of benefit for the future. Only in these terms can Jesus' brief span of life be accurately assessed. He did not travel widely, nor did He head a great movement. But He left twelve apostles who did, after Pentecost, project a movement that has circled the globe and reached every nation of the world. This is the true measure of Jesus' success.

A. *The Preparation.* "That they should be with him."

A call to preach implies a call to prepare. Before the apostles could go out to represent Jesus they must spend time with Him and learn His spirit.

In these days when most professions demand years of preparation, it is difficult to understand how so many can take lightly a call to the ministry. If one would be a lawyer he must go not only to college but to law school. Is winning souls to Christ less important business than winning cases in court? One who chooses to be a physician or surgeon must submit to a very expensive, sacrificial period of training in medical school. Is the cure of souls less important than the cure of bodies? One who takes seriously his call to the ministry will give careful attention to the matter of adequate preparation. For the Christian ministry the seminary is equivalent to what the schools of law and medicine are for those professions.

It should not be overlooked, however, that the most important preparation is a close and enriching fellowship with Christ himself. Nothing else will take the place of this.

B. *The Preaching.* "And that he might send them forth to preach."

What is preaching? To answer that question one would have to note the different Greek verbs translated "preach" in English. One is *euangelizo,* which means "announce good news." Our word "evangelize" is simply a transliteration of it. So in one sense preaching is evangelizing.

The word in our present text is *keryssein*. In the ancient armies of Greece and Rome the *keryx* was the herald who was sent out before the troops to make important proclamations. The word was also used for the herald of the emperor or king.

To the first readers of Mark's Gospel, then, *keryssein* would mean "proclaim." The twelve apostles were to be the heralds of Jesus, going out to proclaim His message. They were the official heralds of the King, making the proclamations that He gave them. They were not representing themselves, but Him. This is what every minister must remember. He is but a herald, speaking for another. It is not his own message he gives, but the King's. What a privilege and what a responsibility!

C. *The Power*. "And to have power to heal sicknesses, and to cast out demons."

Many today would discount the reality of demons. But missionaries working in darkened pagan lands testify to the fact of demon-possession in our time. Some have given reliable reports of casting out demons in the name of Jesus. Where this is needed we cannot doubt that divine authority is available for the situation.

Divine healing has been largely neglected by the church of Christ in modern times. But of late there has been a considerable revival of interest in this subject, even among the leading denominations in the British Isles and the United States. Clergymen in the Anglican Church and the Church of Scotland are reporting miraculous cases of divine healing.

There is another important aspect of which we have only recently become aware. Now that doctors are claiming that perhaps more than half the illness today is psychosomatic, it is being increasingly recognized that the physician needs the services of the minister in the healing of mankind. Here is a great field where the alert pastor can exercise a helpful ministry to the sick.

Mark 4

A QUARTET OF HUMAN HEARTS

4:9. "He that hath ears to hear, let him hear."

I. HISTORICAL SETTING. After Jesus' selection of the Twelve He was so beset with crowds that He and His disciples could not even find opportunity to eat. His relatives said, "He's gone crazy." The scribes had another verdict: "By the prince of demons he is casting out demons." Jesus warned them that they were blaspheming against the Holy Spirit, and thus committing the unpardonable sin.

Meanwhile His relatives had arrived to take Him home and see that He got something to eat. But Jesus met their demands by asserting that His real family consisted of those who "do the will of God" (3:35).

II. EXPOSITORY MEANING. "Sea" in the Gospels almost always means the Lake of Galilee. To those who lived on its shores and fished its waters it was "the sea." "Ship" should be "boat," as any Navy man would be quick to point out! Jesus sat in a small fishing boat, while the crowds gathered on the gentle slope along the shore. It was His favorite setting for teaching.

"Stony" (v. 5) is better rendered "rocky." It refers to thin soil on a ledge of rock, not to ground covered with small stones. "Thorns" may be translated "thistles." "Offended" (v. 17) means "caused to stumble" (*skandalizo*), or "fall away." "Lusts" should be translated "desires." The Greek word does not, of itself, carry any bad connotation.

III. DOCTRINAL VALUE. The emphasis of this parable is on the fact that the effectiveness of the message depends to a great extent on the attitude of the listener. All the seed is good. It is the difference in the kinds of soil that is the point of the parable. For this reason it is sometimes called The

Parable of the Soils. Also one notes the clear implication that some may receive the word and "endure for a time" (v. 17) or even grow up (v. 7) and yet finally be choked out. It is a solemn warning against *a false sense* of "eternal security" that breeds a fatal attitude of complacency in the Christian life.

IV. PRACTICAL AIM. There are two main lessons suggested in this parable. One is that many hearers of the Word receive no profit because of their carelessness (roadside) or callousness (rocky ground), while others grow, but finally allow *things* (thorns) to choke out the spiritual life. The second lesson is that even the good ground brings forth in varying degrees (v. 20). It is a challenge to bear abundant fruit (cf. John 15:2, 5).

V. HOMILETICAL FORM

Theme: "A Quartet of Human Hearts."

Introduction: Every human being catalogs himself. He chooses his own place in the classification of men. There is only one thing we cannot choose — to remain unclassified.

One day a great crowd gathered on the shore of the Lake of Galilee. So dense was the throng that Jesus had to embark in a boat. In keeping with the Jewish custom of His day, He sat while He taught.

Perhaps at that very moment a man strode across a field nearby, taking handfuls of seed from a bag slung over his shoulder and scattering it broadside with wide sweeps of his arm. Pointing to this familiar sight, Jesus said to the crowd on the hillside: "Listen! See! The sower went out to sow." As the crowd turned to look, He called attention to what was happening to the seed. Some fell along the path, some on rocky ground, some among thorns, and some on good soil. "This," said Jesus, "is what is happening to my teaching."

A. *The Stolid Heart.* "Some fell by the way side."

We need to guard against letting our hearts become beaten down into a hard road by the deadly monotony of daily living. We must fence our lives around with care and prayer lest they be trodden and trampled by the legitimate things of life until we lose that receptivity to the Word of God and sensitivity to the presence of the Spirit which alone can save us. There is a great deal of traffic traveling over us every day. Even church services, if we do not keep our hearts responsive, can leave us increasingly insensitive to spiritual things.

B. *The Shallow Heart.* "Some fell on rocky ground."

Some people respond to the message with emotional enthusiasm. But they do not put down their roots in deep repentance, based on a godly sorrow for sin. They live thin lives spiritually. These rootless Christians, with shallow souls, under tribulation or persecution, fall away. Sometimes the people who shed the most tears and show the most emotion are the least stable. Moral endurance is more important than emotional enthusiasm.

C. *The Strangled Heart.* "Some fell among thorns."

1. The cares of this world ("the anxieties of the age").

The cluttering cares of our daily doings can strangle the spiritual life. This is the greatest threat to every Christian. Too busy to pray, too busy to take time to be holy. Choked, starved, dead!

2. The deceitfulness of riches.

Most Americans think that money spells happiness. But riches are deceitful. We spend all our time and energy accumulating them, and they sell us short. Very few wealthy people are happy. Too many say: "When I have made some money, I'll take time for God and the church." But they do not!

3. The desire for other things.

This is the greatest threat to the average Christian. We may allow our lives to become over-crowded with *things* until they choke out the consciousness of God. The radio, the telephone, television, neon signs — all clamor constantly for our attention.

Luccock tells of a schoolboy reading a list of causes of death. He recognized heart failure, cancer, etc., but the last he could not pronounce. So he spelled it out. It was "miscellaneous"! Too often that is the cause of spiritual death.

D. *The Steady Heart.* "Other fell on good ground."

Note the difference in fruitbearing: 30-60-100. Are we functioning at our full capacity? Are we bearing "more fruit" and even "much fruit" (John 15) ?

Where do we find ourselves in this fourfold classification of human hearts?

Mark 4

LITTLE IS MUCH IF GOD IS IN IT

4:30, 31. "The kingdom of God . . . is like a grain of mustard seed."

I. HISTORICAL SETTING. The Gospel of Mark has only four parables, as against fifteen in Matthew and nineteen in Luke. (John has none.) Three of these parables are found in the fourth chapter, and they are all related to sowing seed. After the parable of the sower (4:1-20) comes that of the seed growing secretly (4:26-29). "Of herself" (v. 28) is *automate,* from which we get "automatic." The lesson of this parable is that we must trust the Word of God, when faithfully sown, to take root and grow automatically. We are not to dig up the seed to see if it actually is growing, but trust God's promise: "So shall my word be that goeth forth out of my mouth: it shall not return unto me void, but it shall accomplish that which I please, and it shall prosper in the thing whereto I sent it" (Isa. 55:11). It is possible for Christian workers to get too impatient and not give the seed time to grow.

II. EXPOSITORY MEANING. The third parable is that of the mustard seed, which we are now studying. "With what comparison shall we compare it?" is literally "With what shall we place it in a parable?" The word parable is from the Greek *parabole,* used here. It comes from *para,* "beside," and *ballo,* "throw." So it means something thrown beside another for the purpose of comparison. "Fowls" is better rendered "birds." Today we use the term "fowl" mainly for a domesticated creature with wings, although there is a holdover of the earlier usage in such names as waterfowl.

III. DOCTRINAL VALUE. God is the author of all life. Scientists can analyze the chemical properties of a seed and assemble a synthetic one. But it is doubtful if they will ever be able to put into that artificial seed the germ of life that will make it grow. God is the author of all life. Man can make marvelous things that would seem sheer miracles only a few years ago. Men can make machines. But only God can make a man. That is what our proud age needs humbly to recognize.

IV. PRACTICAL AIM. We need to recognize the importance of sowing the seed and then trusting God for the harvest from our sowing. We also need to believe that small beginnings can produce great results.

V. HOMILETICAL FORM
   Theme: "Little Is Much if God Is in It."
Introduction: This old proverb finds striking illustration in the parable of the mustard seed. The least of all seeds becomes the greatest of all plants. This has been demonstrated thousands of times in the history of the Christian church. We need to believe that it can still be true in our day and in our particular situation.

   A. *Lost in the Soil.* "When it is sown in the earth."
Seed cannot grow unless it is sown. It can be left indefinitely in a dry atmosphere without germinating. Only when it is placed in the ground does it come to life.

So it is with the Word of God. The Bible may lie on the living room table for years without having any effect on the home. But let someone begin to read it with an open mind and honest heart, and something is bound to happen. This has taken place many times both in so-called Christian homes and in pagan lands. Cases are on record of nationals, who had never seen a white missionary, purchasing a Bible from a native colporteur, reading it, and becoming wonderfully saved from sin without ever hearing a Christian sermon.

Jesus said: "Except a corn of wheat fall into the ground and die, it abideth alone: but if it die, it bringeth forth much fruit" (John 12:24). His own death on the cross is the greatest illustration of this truth. He did not win many faithful followers during His lifetime. But His crucifixion has produced a crop of millions of redeemed souls.

In a very real sense this must be true of us as Christian workers. We must die to self that we may be fully alive to

God. We must lose ourselves in sacrificial service if we would find ourselves in the saving of souls.

B. *Least of the Seeds.* "Less than all the seeds."

The mustard seed is not the smallest seed known to botanists. But it was the smallest in common use among the Jews. Already it had become proverbial for something tiny (cf. Matt. 17:20).

The beginnings of the Christian church seemed hopelessly small. Twelve apostles; one hundred twenty Spirit-filled disciples — how could these conquer the world? But within thirty years the gospel of Jesus Christ had swept around the Mediterranean from Jerusalem to Rome. Within a century it compassed the Roman Empire.

Other small beginnings could be cited: the Protestant Reformation in the town of Wittenburg, the Evangelical Revival in the Aldersgate Street experience of John Wesley, the great foreign missionary movement in the courage and faith of William Carey, the American missionary enterprise in the famous haystack prayer meeting. These are only a few among many. We need to trust God that our tiny mustard seed of faith will grow into a great plant of fulfilment.

C. *Largest of the Herbs.* "Greater than all herbs."

Mustard plants have been known to grow to a height of twelve feet or more — all from a little seed. What a parable of the Christian Church! From a despised crowd of "heretics" it has become the greatest enterprise on earth, invading every continent and country for Christ. The kingdom of God has today become the greatest single force on earth, even though seriously threatened by Communism and paganism. Its influence reaches into every nation of the world. Who can recount its conquests?

The individual experience of every Christian also demonstrates this truth in miniature. From the small beginnings of repentance and faith the seed of God's Word grows into a large, beautiful plant of Christian character.

Mark 4

WITH THE MASTER ON BOARD

4:39. "And he arose, and rebuked the wind, and said unto the sea, Peace, be still. And the wind ceased, and there was a great calm."

I. HISTORICAL SETTING. After recounting three parables of Jesus on seed sowing, Mark notes that He spoke "many such parables" to the people (v. 33). At this time He apparently used the parabolic method exclusively with the crowds, reserving for the disciples the explanation of meanings (v. 34).

That evening Jesus decided to get away from the crowds and cross to the east side of the Lake of Galilee (v. 35). There He and His disciples could hope to find the solitude they needed after the busy days near Capernaum. So they entered a boat (not "ship"!), probably Peter's fishing craft, and set out for the other side. This is the first of five withdrawals of Jesus described by Mark.

II. EXPOSITORY MEANING. "Storm" (v. 37) is a strong term in the original. It means "hurricane." The verb "beat" is in the imperfect tense. The waves "were crashing" into the boat. "Full" is obviously a mistranslation. If the boat were actually full, it would have sunk! No boat can be full of water and still stay on the surface. The Greek here clearly says "already filling," which is quite another matter. "Hinder part" (v. 38) is one word, as our "stern." The "pillow" was probably the cushion on the oarsman's seat. Small boats were steered by an oar, as can still be seen on the Nile River. "Master" is literally "teacher." "Arose" (v. 39) might be translated "having been fully wakened." It is a compound of the simple verb "awake" in verse 38. "Peace" is literally "Be silent!" The command "be still" is a strong word. The full meaning is "Be muzzled and stay muzzled" (perfect tense). It would be equivalent to our saying "Shut your mouth and keep it shut!" Perhaps the simplest English translation is, "Keep still!"

III. DOCTRINAL VALUE. All of these miracles of Jesus were demonstrations of His deity. He who created the elements can control them.

The tendency today is to give more credence to Jesus' healing miracles, explaining them often in terms of psychotherapy. That is, it is said that Christ possessed a superior understanding of the psychosomatic nature of most illnesses and cured them by powerful suggestion. At the same time, His nature miracles are called into question. The present one, for instance, is explained as a quieting of the disciples' fears by His firm faith in the care of a loving heavenly Father.

The crux of the problem of miracles is the acceptance of the deity of Jesus and the fact of the Incarnation. Granted that He was the eternal Son of God, no serious problem exists. The Incarnation was the great miracle which makes all lesser miracles not only possible but natural.

IV. PRACTICAL AIM. The Master who stilled the storm on the Lake of Galilee can quiet the tempest in the human heart. Conversely, if we have experienced this stilling of the storm within, we have no difficulty in believing that Jesus could calm the winds and waves of the lake.

V. HOMILETICAL FORM
Theme: "With the Master on Board."

Introduction: Jesus was weary, almost worn out, with his much work on the west side of the Lake of Galilee. Day after day, week after week, the throngs had crowded around Him. He had been constantly busy with teaching, preaching, and healing.

So one day He said to His disciples: "Let us go to the other side of the lake." On the east side it was quiet, relatively uninhabited. There amid the silent hills they could find rest, relaxation, refreshment of body and mind.

A. *The Storm.* "There arose a great storm."

As the little fishing boat pulled out from the western shore Jesus lay down on the steerman's cushion in the stern. There He was soon sound asleep. The measure of His weariness is shown by the fact that He did not even waken when the wind began to blow and the water became rough.

At first it was just a gentle breeze. Then suddenly the storm struck. Wind off the highland plateau on the east side of the lake rushed down the canyons which acted as funnels, hitting the surface of the water with terrifying fury. Quickly the fishermen furled their sail and tied it tightly to the mast. But the waves were breaking over the bow and the boat was filling fast. Finally, afraid for their lives, these hardy sailors rushed back to Jesus, shook Him awake and cried: "Teacher, is it not a care to you that we are perishing!"

B. *The Sternness.* "And he arose, and rebuked the wind, and said unto the sea, Peace, be still."

Jesus' reaction was immediate and mighty. The Master of earth and sea and sky stood to His feet. Looking into the teeth of the howling hurricane He uttered just two words: "Silence! Keep still!"

From anyone else's lips that would have been sheer insanity. But when God — Father, Son, or Holy Spirit — speaks, the word has divine authority and infinite power. This was not an empty gesture. It was the act of the Creator who was conscious of control of His own creation.

The sternness with which Jesus "rebuked" the wind is noted. It was as if He said: "What do you mean by terrifying my disciples while I am resting? Hush up! Put the muzzle on and keep it on! Not another sound out of you!"

What a comforting thought! When Jesus is on board our frail bark we never need to fear. He is the Commander who can take us safely across life's sea to our eternal harbor home.

C. *The Stillness.* "And the wind ceased, and there was a great calm."

The winds ceased their raging, and the waves stopped their rolling. As they sank to restful slumber, a dead calm ensued. To one who has had the storm of sin stilled in his soul there is no problem in believing that Jesus could quiet the tempest on the lake. The former is a greater miracle than the latter.

No matter how furious the storms of life that may beset us, if we turn to the Master we can always hear His quieting command, "Peace, be still."

Mark 5

PUBLIC ENEMY NO. 1

5:3-5. "had his dwelling among the tombs . . . neither could any man tame him . . . crying, and cutting himself with stones."

I. HISTORICAL SETTING. When Jesus and His disciples arrived on the east side of the lake they expected to find a quiet place of rest. Instead they found a raging maniacal demoniac. Jesus had to perform another miracle, stilling the storm in this deranged man's mind. But He was equal to the occasion.

II. EXPOSITORY MEANING. There is a bit of problem about the variant readings (v. 1) : Gadarenes, Gerasenes, and Gergesenes. The first would refer to the largest city nearby, Gadara, which was half a dozen miles from the southern tip of the lake. Gerasa and Gergesa may both stand for the village of Khersa, the ruins of which have been discovered on the eastern shore of Galilee. "Crying" (v. 5) does not mean weeping but "crying out" or screaming. "Devils" (v. 12) should be "demons." The Greek always makes a clear distinction between one devil (*diabolos,* always singular) and many demons (*daimonia*). The difference should be maintained in English.

III. DOCTRINAL VALUE. The main problem that confronts us here is the doctrine of demonology. The tendency today is to dismiss the idea as merely a superstitious way the ancients had of explaining the phenomena of insanity. It is true that demon-possession and insanity are often linked together in the Gospels. Most demoniacs were maniacs. But this solution is too simple to be true. Many modern scholars are feeling that the happenings in our world today can be explained only on the basis of unseen forces of evil at work in human beings. The Bible calls them demons, and the evidence of their existence is abundant and obvious.

IV. PRACTICAL AIM. No matter how sad and seemingly hopeless a man's condition, divine power can set him completely free from the awful bondage of sin. What men need is to meet Jesus. He can cure every case.

V. HOMILETICAL FORM

Theme: "Public Enemy No. 1."

Introduction: Jesus and His disciples beached their boat on the eastern shore and stepped out on solid ground. Now they would enjoy the quiet rest they sought.

But suddenly the silence of the solitude was shattered by piercing shrieks. Looking up the hill they saw an awful apparition — half man, half monster. Naked, disheveled, dirty, he came rushing down upon them, while his horrible screams rent the air.

The disciples turned to run to the boat and push out from the shore for safety. But seeing the same stern look on Jesus' face with which He had faced the raging storm on the lake a short time before, they paused and watched. When the demoniac's eyes met the Master's, he stopped, and then fell trembling on his face. Then it was that Jesus commanded the unclean spirit to come out of him.

In the description of the Gadarene demoniac we have a vivid picture of sin, which is public enemy number 1. We might note some of the lines of that portrait.

A. *Sin is Suicide.* "Had his dwelling among the tombs."

This man was literally living in the place of death, and liking it. He felt more at home there.

Everyone who is not believing in Jesus Christ as his Savior is dwelling in the place of death (John 3:36). The person who keeps on sinning is slowly but surely committing spiritual suicide. The Bible declares: "The wages of sin is death" (Rom. 6:23). Every time a man deliberately disobeys God he is driving another nail into the coffin of his eternal doom.

B. *Sin is Insanity.* "Neither could any man tame him."

When the maniac had his quieter moments the men of the nearby village would seize him, fasten his hands with chains behind his back, then quickly tie ropes tightly around his ankles. But soon the demoniac forces within would assert themselves. He would tear the chains apart, kick the fetters off his feet, and rush at his captors with murderous fury.

Sin is *unbindable*. You can bind it down in one place, and it will break forth in another. You can conquer one habit, and another will get the best of you. You cannot conquer sin! Only Christ can.

Also sin is *untamable*. It is a wild monster which no man can tame. Only God can solve the problem of sin. It is claimed that a bear is the most treacherous creature in the north woods. You cannot trust it. You may think you have it tamed, and it will turn on you. Sin is like that.

C. *Sin is Self-destruction.* "And always, night and day, he was in the mountains, and in the tombs, crying out, and cutting himself with stones."

Wandering among the tombs, the demoniac would pick up the sharp stones of the hillside and slash himself, until the blood was running down his naked body and caking with the filth and perspiration there.

What a sordid sight! But no worse than that of the sinner who slashes his soul. We can see the effects outwardly of such sins of the flesh as drunkenness. The sunken cheeks, hollow eyes, red nose, trembling fingers, staggering step, weakened will — all these tell their sad tale of self-destruction. But the sins of the flesh are no less damaging. Anger, hate, jealousy, pride — they, too, take their toll. These destroy the finer fiber of the soul just as truly as the sins of the flesh destroy the body. All sin is self-destruction.

Mark 5

FAITH RECEIVING

5:34. "thy faith hath made thee whole."

I. HISTORICAL SETTING. After he had been healed the Gadarene demoniac wanted to follow Jesus. This was a natural expression of his gratitude. But instead the Master commanded him to go home and tell his friends what had happened to him. The man gladly obeyed, and so the news of Jesus' power spread throughout the Decapolis. Thus the way was prepared for Jesus' later ministry there (7:31).

By boat Jesus and His disciples returned to the west side of the lake. There a synagogue ruler named Jairus asked Him to hurry to the bedside of his dying daughter. On the way there occurred the incident of our present study.

II. EXPOSITORY MEANING. "Issue" (v. 25) means "flowing." "Press" (v. 27) is "crowd." The word for "garment" is *himation,* the outer garment or robe. "Whole" (v. 28) is literally "saved." The verb *sozo* is used of physical healing in the Gospels and spiritual salvation in the Epistles. In Acts it is used both ways. "Virtue" (v. 30) is "power" (*dynamis*). It is interesting to note that Jesus was conscious of power having gone out of Him in response to the woman's faith. "Thronging thee" (v. 31) is literally "pressing you together." In verse 34 the first "whole" is "saved" (*sozo*). But the second is an entirely different word, *hygies,* from which comes "hygiene." In the Pastoral Epistles this word is translated "sound" (e.g., sound doctrine).

III. DOCTRINAL VALUE. The deity and humanity of Jesus are beautifully blended here. The Master was conscious that divine energy had gone from Him to heal the woman. Yet He asked, "Who touched my clothes?" and kept looking around to see who it was. When she had confessed, He assured her that her faith had resulted in her healing, and He bade her go in peace.

IV. PRACTICAL AIM. To show that if we come to Jesus in simple, child-like faith we know He will meet our need. Also, to suggest the importance of testifying to what Christ has done for us.

V. HOMILETICAL FORM

Theme: "Faith Receiving."

Introduction: We have here a unique incident in the Gospels: two miracles dovetailed in together. Jesus starts for the house of Jairus to heal the latter's daughter. On the way the woman touches Him, receives healing, and testifies to it. Then Jesus continues on to the synagogue ruler's house and raises his daughter. We have a suggestion, in symbol, of two necessary phases of soul-winning. Some sinners will come to the church and be saved. But others will have to be reached in their homes, or not at all. Again, some sinners come to Jesus for help, while others seem helpless to make a move toward Him. As in the case of Jairus' daughter, they must have the Master brought to them.

A. *The Woman's Affliction.* "An issue of blood twelve years."

The life is in the blood. When one's blood is constantly flowing, life and strength are ebbing away. This had gone on in the woman's case for twelve long years.

The situation was aggravated by the fact that her condition was apparently hopeless. With the uninhibited frankness of a layman, Mark records the sad story: She "had suffered many things of many physicians, and had spent all that she had, and was nothing bettered, but rather grew worse" (v. 26). Luke the physician describes it in a way that protected his profession. He admits she "had spent all her living upon physicians," but adds "neither could be healed of any" (8:43). In other words, hers was an incurable case.

Mark's statement that she had "suffered many things from many physicians" finds ample illustration in what we know about Jewish doctors of that day. The rabbis had a saying: "The best physician is worthy of Gehenna." It is still the

custom in some places of the East to call in as many physicians as possible, with sad results for the patient. The methods
used were often both cruel and useless. For a further description of Jewish medicine in that day see Adam Clarke (V, 304)
or Vincent's *Word Studies* (I, 189). Mark has not expressed
the matter one bit too strongly. Her medical treatment had
caused untold suffering and not benefited her at all. She was
discouraged, with all hope gone.

B. *The Woman's Faith.* "If I may touch but his clothes, I
shall be whole."

In her helpless, hopeless condition the woman heard about
the healing miracles of Jesus ("heard of Jesus" is in the best
Greek text "heard the things concerning Jesus"). Hope sprang
up within her. Perhaps He can heal me too! So she came as
fast as her weakened condition would permit. Her loss of
blood had naturally made her timid and easily embarrassed
in public. So she slipped through the crowd as unobtrusively
as possible, came behind Jesus, and reached out to touch His
garment.

C. *The Woman's Fortune.* "She was healed."

It was just that quick! "Straightway" the flow of blood was
stopped. She knew she was well. With what a thrill of joy
she must have turned to leave. She would escape as unnoticed
as she had come.

But Jesus wanted to confer upon her an added blessing, one
that could only come as she met Him face to face and thanked
Him. No blessing is quite complete without the response of
gratitude. It was not heartless cruelty that caused Jesus to
make the woman identify herself and testify publicly. It was
His love that wanted to lift her to a higher level. No longer
need she sneak around out of sight, ashamed to be seen in
public. Hers was to be a new life, and He wished her to begin
it right then and there. It was worth it all to hear from His
own lips, "Go in peace." Her heart, as well as her body, was
healed that day.

Mark 5

FAITH THAT KNOWS NO FAILURE

5:36. "Be not afraid, only believe."

I. HISTORICAL SETTING. It is altogether possible that Jairus' daughter had become ill while Jesus was across the lake in the country of the Gadarenes. If so, we may well imagine the eager concern with which the distressed father awaited the return of the great Healer. As soon as he heard that Jesus had arrived on the west side of the lake he hurried out to the shore to meet Him. By now the crowds had gathered (v. 21). But Jairus pushed his way forward to the Teacher and begged Him to come immediately to his home.

II. EXPOSITORY MEANING. The "other side" (v. 21) means Capernaum (Matt. 9:1). Jesus was back home again in "his own city." A ruler of the synagogue (v. 22) was the president, who presided but did not teach or preach. This was done by the rabbis. The synagogue president, as today, was a layman. "Lieth at the point of death" (v. 23) might more literally be translated: "is at her last gasp." "Heard" (v. 36) is in the best Greek text "ignored" (*parakousas* instead of *akousas*). The latter is the common meaning of the compound (cf. ASV). "Be not afraid" (v. 36) is literally "stop being afraid" (present imperative). "Only believe" is "just keep on believing" (also present imperative). "Tumult" (v. 38) means "uproar." "Make ye this ado" (v. 39) is the same root as "tumult" (v. 38). So we might better render it "make an uproar." That will show the connection of the two words in the Greek. "Talitha cumi" (v. 41) is Aramaic, the language of the common people of Palestine in that day. "Straitly" (v. 43) is simply "much."

III. DOCTRINAL VALUE. As in the healing of the woman with a hemorrhage, dovetailed in between the two sections of the raising of Jairus' daughter, we observe both Jesus' love and His power in action. His acts of power were always expressions of His nature of love. It is still so today. There is the further suggestion that God always honors faith.

IV. PRACTICAL AIM. To learn that love never lets us down; that though our faith may be tested, it is for our highest good; that when things seem to be getting worse, God can get greater glory in the victory that finally comes.

V. HOMILETICAL FORM

Theme: "Faith That Knows No Failure."

Introduction: The position of Jairus as president of the synagogue made him one of the most respected members of the community. In view of the attitude of the Jewish leaders toward Jesus, it may not have been an easy thing for him to seek out the help of the prophet from Nazareth. But desperation knows no barriers, and love has no limits. So the ruler came and fell at Jesus' feet in abject humility and earnest supplication. He "besought him greatly" (v. 23) to come and heal his daughter.

A. *Faith Trying.* "Come . . . that she may be healed."

Real faith always produces action. Without works, says James, faith is dead. Jairus showed his faith in Jesus' healing power by coming to Him in his hour of greatest need. The rabbis of his own synagogue could give no help, but he believed that Jesus could.

His faith is shown not only by his action but also by his words. He asked Jesus to come and lay His hands on the little girl "in order that she may be saved and live" (literal translation). He would not have asked had he not believed.

B. *Faith Tried.* "Be not afraid, only believe."

As Jesus and the anxious father hurried toward the house where the little girl lay dying, the people thronged around them and impeded their progress. We can imagine Jairus already getting impatient at being slowed down.

But the worst was yet to come. A woman touched Jesus' clothes and was healed. The Master stopped, turned around, and asked who touched Him. Why was that necessary? Not only that, but He kept on looking around, seeking to discover who had touched Him. Finally the woman came forward and gave a full testimony to what had happened. Jesus gently assured her that her faith had made her whole, and bade her go in peace.

Meanwhile some messengers from Jairus' house hurried up to him and said — so Jesus could hear! — "Your daughter has died; why bother him? He doesn't care! If he had, he would not have been fooling around talking to this woman. If he cared anything about your daughter, he would have come straight to the house without delay. It's too late now!"

Imagine how Jairus felt. Could he have any more faith in Jesus now? But the Master, ignoring the slurring tones of the messengers' voices, quietly commanded: "Stop being afraid; keep on believing." It was Jairus' darkest hour. But faith met the test. He did not angrily turn away from Jesus, but led Him to the house.

C. *Faith Triumphant.* "The damsel arose."

When Jesus arrived at the home, He found a confused uproar. The hired professional mourners were already making a loud noise weeping and wailing — the louder the better they were paid. It was no kind of an atmosphere for the exercise of faith.

So Jesus put them all out. Taking the father and mother and His inner circle of three disciples, He entered the room where the girl lay dead. Taking her by the hand He spoke in the familiar Aramaic perhaps the very words with which the mother was in the habit of calling her daughter in the morning. The girl opened her eyes, got up, and walked. Faith had not failed! What a joyous victory celebration it was for Jairus. But the parents must feed the restored life. Divine miracles do not rule out human responsibility.

Mark 6

A KING'S UNEASY CONSCIENCE

6:16. "It is John, whom I beheaded."

I. HISTORICAL SETTING. After Jesus had raised Jairus'
daughter he left Capernaum and came into "his own country"
— Nazareth. Here He taught in the synagogue on the Sabbath.
His fellow townsmen were astonished at His teaching and
miracle-working power, but they stumbled ("offended," *skandalizo,* v. 3) over the fact that He was known to them as the
village "carpenter." The sad thing was that Jesus was hin-
dered from blessing them with His healing ministry, because
of their unbelief.

The Master then sent out His twelve apostles on a preaching mission throughout Galilee. Their proclamation (*kerysso,*
v. 12) was that men should "repent." Herod heard of Jesus'
miraculous ministry, and immediately his conscience began
to trouble him.

II. EXPOSITORY MEANING. Herod is called "king" (v.
14). Actually he was only a tetrarch, ruler of Galilee and
Perea. His father, Herod the Great, had been king of all
Palestine. But at his death the kingdom was divided among
his sons. However, Herod Antipas was popularly called "king."
In fact, the Romans — and Mark was writing in Rome —
tended to call all Eastern rulers kings. Matthew and Luke
give him his more correct title of tetrarch. Herod Antipas
ruled from 4 B. C. to A. D. 39.

While on a visit to Rome, Antipas stayed in the home of
his brother Philip. There he fell in love with his brother's
wife, Herodias (v. 17). She forsook her husband and accompanied Antipas to Galilee. But John the Baptist cried out
against this ungodly situation. The result was that Herodias

"had a quarrel against him" (v. 19) . The Greek literally says, "had it in for him."

"Observed" (v. 20) is more accurately translated "was keeping him safe" — from Herodias' attempts to asassinate him? For "did many things" the oldest manuscripts have "was much perplexed." The "charger" (v. 25) was not a horse, but a "platter." The meaning of "by and by" is just the opposite today from its use here (KJV) . The Greek word means "immediately." "Sat" (v. 26) is "reclined." The custom in those days was to recline on cushioned couches while eating and drinking. "Executioner" (v. 27) means one of Herod's body guard. "His disciples" would be the followers of John the Baptist (cf. John 1:35) .

III. DOCTRINAL VALUE. Two doctrines are illustrated in this lesson: the awful depravity of the human heart, and the conscience as monitor of the soul.

IV. PRACTICAL AIM. To show that one cannot escape the voice of conscience speaking within. Also that God may allow seeming tragedy to take place, but will cause it all to work out for the progress of His kingdom.

V. HOMILETICAL FORM
   Theme: "A King's Uneasy Conscience."
   Introduction: Herod had killed the preacher. But he found he still had a powerful preacher inside, whose voice he could not silence. Conscience rose up to haunt him with memories from the past. He found that while he could get rid of John he could not escape himself. He had to live with himself as the bloody murderer who had killed a righteous man.

   A. *Cutting Conscience.* "It is John, whom I beheaded."

   When Herod Antipas heard about the miracles Jesus was performing, his conscience took a sudden twist, cutting him to the quick. "It is John," he cried out, "John whom I beheaded."

   Superstitious as he was, Antipas did not doubt that John the Baptist had "risen from the dead." No one else could be doing the things that Jesus was doing. It must be John.

   Herod was a weak, vacillating character. That is indicated

by the correct reading of verse 20. He was "perplexed," upset, at his wit's end. But like Jezebel with her Ahab, so Herodias cast her evil spell over Herod and led him on to his doom.

Criminals pay an awful price for their crime. The worst penalty is not the fine or prison sentence, but the gnawing accusation of conscience. What a wonderful blessing to live with a conscience "void of offense"!

B. *Crafty Conniving.* "Herodias had it in for him."

There is nothing in the world more cruel than a crafty woman. One is reminded of Madame Defarge in *The Tale of Two Cities,* knitting away while she plotted against scores of men and saw them sent to the guillotine.

They say that a woman never forgets. Herodias never forgave John the Baptist for implying that she was an adulteress. She made up her mind to get him. And she did!

She found "a convenient day" (v. 21) when her husband's birthday arrived. Doubtless she worked hard to make as elaborate preparations as possible. She wanted her revenge on the prophet to be as public as she could make it.

We may be sure that she saw to it that the king drank heavily. It was important that he be drunk enough to fall in with her plans and make a rash promise.

C. *Cruel Compliance.* "The daughter . . . danced."

The most important piece of strategy that Herodias planned was this: when Herod and his men were so sodden with drink that their passions could be most completely roused, Herodias' daughter Salome would come in and put on a very sensuous dance in front of the men. Of course it was unheard of that a princess should perform like a common slave girl. But so desperate was Herodias that she was willing to degrade and disgrace her own daughter publicly in order to win her purpose.

The sad thing is that Salome complied. How she must have winced as she took the bloody head on the platter to her mother. But nothing was too low to stoop to if only John could be killed. So the degenerate daughter carried the bloody gift to the murderous mother, and human hate was satiated with the sacrifice.

Mark 6

THE REWARD OF OBEDIENCE

6:37. "Give ye them to eat."

I. HISTORICAL SETTING. The twelve whom Jesus had sent forth (v. 7) now returned (v. 30). They reported the miracles they had wrought (cf. v. 13) and the teaching they had given.

The Master realized that His men needed a vacation after their strenuous preaching mission. There was no opportunity for this on the western shore. In fact, the crowds thronged them so constantly that they could not even find leisure to eat (v. 31). So Jesus said to them: "Come ye yourselves apart into a desert place, and rest awhile." The little group embarked in a boat and headed across the lake to find a quiet spot. But the people recognized Jesus, as the boat pulled out, and hurried on foot around the north end of the lake, reaching the landing place before the disciples arrived.

II. EXPOSITORY MEANING. "Desert place" (v. 35) means deserted place, or lonely spot, not a sandy waste. "Pennyworth" (v. 37) is *denarii*. A denarius was worth about twenty cents, but represented a day's wages. "Sit down" (v. 39) is "recline." The Greek "by companies" is *"symposia, symposia,"* from which our word "symposium" comes. The Greek for "in ranks" is *"prasiai, prasiai."* It means "garden beds" and suggests the orderly arrangement of the people. But it also probably reflects Peter's reaction when he saw the people reclining on the green grass in groups, with their bright Oriental garments of red and yellow. They looked to him like flower beds. Mark has retained the vivid picture for us. "Filled" (v. 42) is literally "grassed." It was used of animals being satisfied after grazing, filled with grass. The twelve "baskets" (v. 43) were probably the lunch baskets of the twelve apostles.

"Men" (v. 44) is not the generic term, but means "males." Matthew adds: "besides women and children."

III. DOCTRINAL VALUE. The deity of Jesus is underscored again. The matter of nature miracles comes in once more. Also the compassion of Christ receives forcible emphasis.

IV. PRACTICAL AIM. To show that when God guides He provides, that when He commands us to do anything He will furnish the enablement. Our part is to obey, His to furnish the power.

V. HOMILETICAL FORM

Theme: "The Reward of Obedience."

Introduction: Sometimes God asks us to do the seemingly impossible. Our only responsibility is to obey. On His part He gives divine enablement for the assigned task.

Jesus asked His disciples to do something utterly impossible — feed a crowd of thousands with a single person's little lunch. But they did it! That is the thrilling fact which holds an important lesson for us today.

A. *The Master's Compassion.* "And Jesus, when he came out, saw much people, and was moved with compassion toward them."

It had been planned as a quiet vacation. Jesus and His disciples had left the western shore to get away from the throngs. But the crowd had hurried around the north end of the lake and was waiting for Him when He landed.

One might expect Jesus to react with resentment at the presence of the people. But instead of being irritated, He was gripped with compassion (aorist tense) and taught the eager people. Weary as He was, He knew they needed His help.

B. *The Men's Confusion.* "Send them away."

As evening drew on the disciples became deeply concerned. They had thousands of guests for supper, and nothing to give them. No wonder they pleaded with Jesus: "Send them away!"

To add to their confusion Jesus replied: "You give them to eat." How utterly preposterous! They had nothing. And even if they had half a year's wages, that would not give every one enough.

We must remember that Oriental custom demanded that hospitality be extended to all who were present. To the disciples it was a very embarrassing situation, and they wanted to get out of it as quickly as possible.

The disciples thought they had nothing. But Jesus asked them to make a careful check. Andrew came up with the information that there was a boy there with a small lunch of five loaves and two small fish (cf. John 6:9). The loaves were just mere biscuits, like a small pancake. The two fish were probably the size of sardines, pickled to preserve them. What could one boy's lunch do for that crowd? The disciples were still confused.

C. *The Multitude's Comfort.* "They did all eat, and were filled."

First, Jesus commanded the disciples to have the people recline on the green grass of the hillside in groups of fifty and a hundred. This would facilitate both the counting and the serving. It took some faith on the part of the disciples to carry out these orders. To set the table, ask the guests to sit down, and then have no food for them! But they obeyed.

Then Jesus took the five biscuits and the two little fish, blessed the food, broke it, and distributed it to the twelve disciples. They in turn served the whole crowd. At the close each apostle filled his lunch basket as a sort of tip for his services. This would give them food for the next day.

The lesson here is clear. Jesus said: "You give them to eat." They could not. But when they obeyed the Master, He enabled them to do exactly that. They did feed the crowd. When Christ commands us to do the seemingly impossible it is ours to obey and He will furnish the means.

Mark 6

A PRESENCE IN THE DARKNESS

6:50. "Be of good cheer: it is I; be not afraid."

I. HISTORICAL SETTING. After the feeding of the five thousand — the only miracle of Jesus recorded in all four Gospels — the Master constrained His disciples to get into the boat and head back across the lake. We learn from John's Gospel (6:15) that the people wanted to make Jesus king. A Messiah who could feed five thousand with five loaves would solve all their economic problems!

But Jesus had not come to set up a political kingdom. He sent away the disciples — who would have been delighted to see their Master made king — and then dismissed the crowd. He himself went up a hill to spend the night in prayer. What He desired for Israel was not a political revolution but a spiritual revival.

II. EXPOSITORY MEANING. The location of Bethsaida (v. 45) has caused some dispute. It seems best to take this as the well-known Bethsaida Julias on the east bank of the Jordan River where it enters the Lake of Galilee. The feeding of the five thousand took place a short distance south of Bethsaida (Luke 9:10). The disciples evidently headed across the bay toward Bethsaida, expecting to pick up Jesus there. Instead the storm drove them out into the middle of the lake. There Jesus came to them, walking on the water, and they continued across to Gennesaret (v. 53). This was a small plain on the west side of the lake.

The "fourth watch of the night" (v. 48) would be from 3:00 A. M. to 6:00 A. M. "Toiling" is hardly strong enough to bring out the force of the Greek word. It meant to "examine by torture." So it could be translated "tortured," "tormented," or "distressed." Although the disciples had been rowing for

59

perhaps eight hours they had covered only three or four miles (John 6:19). They were half way across the lake and having a very difficult time. "Would have passed by them" has raised some discussion. The simplest way is to take this as the point of view of an eye-witness. It seemed to the disciples that the figure meant to pass them by.

III. DOCTRINAL VALUE. Again the deity of Jesus is in the foreground. He could walk on the water with no fear.

IV. PRACTICAL AIM. To show that Jesus always comes to us in the hour of our darkest difficulty and greatest need, even though we may not always recognize Him.

V. HOMILETICAL FORM
   Theme: "A Presence in the Darkness."
   Introduction: It was dark. The wind was contrary. The waves were rolling high. Not even the moon shone to relieve the gloom of the night.
   It seemed too bad they could not have crowned Christ king. Then the Messianic Age would dawn. All would be peace and happiness.

   A. *A Sight.* "They saw . . . a spirit."
   To the disciples that night it seemed that everything was against them. They were dejected, disappointed, downhearted. Out in the middle of the lake, unable to reach shore, worn out with rowing against the wind — all this instead of a kingdom.
   Just then someone spotted something on the water. A figure draped in white, it looked like a ghost. They screamed in fear. It was bad enough to have the elements against them. But now to be tormented by a spirit was more than they could take. This was the last straw that broke their jaded nerves. They were terrified.

   B. *A Sound.* "He talked with them."
   What a comfort it was when they heard the familiar voice of the Master. It was not a ghost; it was Jesus! His first words to them were: "Be of good cheer: it is I; be not afraid."
   How often do we fail to recognize Jesus when He comes to us in the dark hours of life? Sometimes the form in which He

approaches us only fills us with greater fear. We do not know Him in the night.

But then He speaks in the still, small voice within our hearts. We hear Him say: "Be of good courage; I am; stop being afraid." Jesus is still walking on the sea of life, visiting us in our distress, and bringing us safely across to the other side.

C. *A Silence*. "The wind ceased."

The raging of the wind, the roar of the crashing waves — all this was gone. Instead there was quiet peace on the Lake of Galilee. We can even imagine that the clouds were pulled back, and the face of the sky could be seen again.

There is nothing more distressing than being tossed and pitched about in a small boat on the water, with no way of escaping. It leaves one with a helpless feeling. On the other hand there is nothing more peaceful than a ship on a quiet sea. In the silence that ensued the disciples felt the comforting presence of their Lord. How they enjoyed the quiet peace of the water as they finished their journey across the lake. We need the storms in order that we may appreciate the calm.

Mark 7

THE SIN OF CEREMONIALISM

7:20. "That which cometh out of the man, that defileth the man."

I. HISTORICAL SETTING. The previous incident in the Gospel is located in the small plain of Gennesaret, on the west side of the Lake of Galilee. Here in villages, cities, and country the people flocked to Jesus again, bringing their sick to be healed, (6:53-56). Presumably the present incident took place in that general area.

II. EXPOSITORY MEANING. "Defiled" (v. 2) is literally "common." To the ceremonially-minded Pharisees common meant unclean. Instead of *pykna* ("oft," v. 3) the best Greek text has *pyme*, which literally means "fist." This has been variously interpreted as "to the wrist" or "up to the elbow." Probably the simplest translation is "diligently" (ERV, ASV). The "tradition of the elders" was a body of oral regulations handed down by the rabbis and later put in written form.

"Washing" (v. 4) is "baptisms." The strict Jews baptized (washed) their cups, pots, and cooking vessels to rid them of all ceremonial defilement. The phrase "and of tables" is not in the oldest manuscripts and should probably be omitted.

The term "hypocrites" (v. 6) comes directly from the Greek *hypocrites* (only here in Mark, 13 times in Matthew, 3 times in Luke, not elsewhere in N.T.). It was originally used for an actor on the stage. Greek and Roman actors wore big masks which concealed small megaphones, in order to be heard by the large audiences. So being a hypocrite means wearing a false face.

The Hebrew word "Corban" means "gift." It was used for gifts devoted to the temple. But in Jesus' day it signified merely an oath or a vow which could not be revoked.

"Purging all meats" (v. 19) is probably an explanation added by the writer of the Gospel (cf. ASV — "This he said, making all meats clean"). That is, the distinction between clean and unclean meats was not to carry over into the Christian dispensation (cf. Acts 10:15).

"Thoughts" (v. 21) is "reasonings" or "designs" (Moffatt). "An evil eye" (v. 22) was the Hebrew phrase for envy. "Blasphemy" is speaking evil of God or man. Probably here it means "slander." The Greek word for pride (only here in N.T.) suggests self-exaltation and looking down with contempt on others. "Foolishness" is more moral than mental. It is the attitude of making sin a joke.

III. DOCTRINAL VALUE. Sin is moral, rather than ceremonial, uncleanness. The latter is the view of most non-Christian religions. It is a false, superficial concept of sin, against which Jesus rebelled deeply. Christianity demands inward and outward rightness. It is the main emphasis of Amos and Micah that true religion is a matter of righteousness, not ritual.

IV. PRACTICAL AIM. To show the importance of inward, moral cleanness.

V. HOMILETICAL FORM
Theme: "The Sin of Ceremonialism."
Introduction: The bane of most religion, including much of "Christianity," is the substitution of ritualism for righteousness. This may be called the sin of ceremonialism — a false righteousness. It was the sin of the Pharisees and Jesus denounced it severely.

A. *The Cleaning of Cups.* "the washing of cups, and pots, brazen vessels."
This was the religion of the Pharisees — at least, to a distressing degree. In the Jewish Mishna thirty chapters are devoted to the cleansing of dishes. Ceremonialism as a substitute for moral cleanness — this was the sin of the Pharisees. Over and over again Jesus emphasized the fact that inward cleansing was more important than outward purifications.

Even the sacrament of baptism can become a meaningless ceremony, with no more spiritual significance than what is here literally called the "baptisms" of cups and pots and pans. Religion must always be a matter of the heart, or it is not true religion.

We find it easy to criticize the Pharisaic obsession with outward things of the flesh. But to keep Christianity today a religion of the spirit is a constant struggle.

B. *The Case of Corban.* "But ye say, If a man shall say to his father or mother, It is Corban . . . he shall be free."

When the Pharisees criticized the disciples for not living (walking) according to the tradition of the elders, Jesus in turn charged them with a far more serious offense — rejecting God's commandment that they might keep their tradition. He cited a specific case. God said, through Moses: "Honor thy father and thy mother." But the rabbis taught that a man might declare as "Corban" what he should have used to support his parents. Having dedicated the money, he could not give it to his father and mother for their needs. But the catch was that he did not need to give it to the temple either. He could keep it for his own use after his parents' death. Both Christian and Jewish writers agree that this was the actual practice.

C. *The Character of Carnality.* "out of the heart of men, proceed evil thoughts."

The Jews taught that eating unclean meat defiled a man. Jesus said an emphatic "No!" Nothing physical defiles a man's spirit. It is the outflowing, outpouring of his carnal nature that defiles him.

The true character of carnality is shown here in all its black ugliness. A man does not become a sinner by committing murder, theft, or adultery. He does these things because he *is* a sinner. Outward sins are only reflections of inward sin, and the sins of the spirit are equally wicked in God's sight.

Mark 7

THE TENDERNESS OF THE MASTER

7:37. "He hath done all things well."

I. HISTORICAL SETTING. After Jesus' bout with the Pharisees He withdrew for a third time (cf. 4:35; 6:31). This time he went north into the territory of Tyre and Sidon. This is the ancient Phoenicia, modern Lebanon, on the coast of Syria. Here a Syrophoenician woman petitioned him to cast a demon out of her daughter. After testing her faith, Jesus granted her request. Then he returned to the east side of the Lake of Galilee. It is obvious that He was carefully avoiding the territory of Herod Antipas, because the latter wanted to kill Him (Luke 13:31).

II. EXPOSITORY MEANING. "Coasts" (v. 31) means "borders." The "Decapolis" was a region of ten cities (*deca polis*). It included Damascus in the far north and Philadelphia (modern Amman) in the south. "Had an impediment in his speech" (v. 32) is all one word in the Greek. It means "speaking with difficulty." The word "Ephphatha" (v. 34) is Aramaic. "Be opened" is a compound — be opened completely. "String" (v. 35) is "bond." It would seem that he was literally tongue-tied. "Plain" is "straight."

III. DOCTRINAL VALUE. Again we see Jesus' divine power displayed in healing an afflicted body. Also we see the tender compassion of the Great Physician, His love matching His power. In fact, His power was love.

IV. PRACTICAL AIM. To give us an example of how thoughtfully and tenderly we should deal with afflicted souls.

V. HOMILETICAL FORM
Theme: "The Tenderness of the Master."
Introduction: We are apt to think of tenderness as weak-

ness. Nothing could be further from the truth! The all-power-ful One was All-Love. Because of that, He was infinitely ten-der in dealing with the needy. To be strong enough to control our powers and use them only for healing and helping — that is the evidence of inward strength. Brusqueness, crudeness, rudeness, roughness — these are signs of weakness. The brag-ging boaster is usually a coward. True strength is found in a combination of sweetness and firmness. This Jesus had.

A. *The Man's Trouble.* "And they bring unto him one that was deaf, and had an impediment in his speech."

One time it was a leper, another time a blind man or a helpless paralytic. Now it was a deaf mute. But the Great Phy-sician was able to cure every case.

It would seem that the man was physically tongue-tied. Not being able to hear himself, he perhaps could not know how pathetic his incoherent mumblings sounded.

Unable to hear a word, not able to make himself under-stood by others — what a lonely life he led! Jesus had com-passion on him and changed everything that day.

B. *The Master's Touch.* "He . . . put his fingers into his ears . . . and touched his tongue."

Note the tender compassion of the Christ: "he took him aside from the multitude." A deaf man is naturally embar-rassed and easily confused. Graciously, thoughtfully Jesus took him aside from the crowd.

With this should be compared the healing of the blind man of Bethsaida (8:22-26), the only other miracle recorded by Mark alone. The two have much in common. Note how gently Jesus took the blind man by the hand and led him outside the city. These men needed to be treated in quiet privacy. There were emotional as well as physical factors to be consid-ered. Often sinners need to be dealt with alone, away from the confusion of a public place.

In both cases Jesus touched the affected spot. With the deaf stammerer it was his ears and tongue. This was a symbol of the cure that was soon to come and was intended to bolster his faith. With the blind man it was his eyes. Unique among

the miracles of the Master, this took place in two stages —
"Twice He touched my blinded eyes."

The clear lesson in these two incidents is that Jesus deals
with each of us as individuals. He knows just how to tailor
the treatment to our specific needs and particular personalities.

C. *The Multitude's Testimony.* "He hath done all things
well."

What a tremendous testimony! Jesus earned it. How far do
we?

It should be noted that a man's spirit is the most important
thing. Not one of us will live without mistakes, as Jesus did.
But we can all, by God's grace, show a good spirit all the time.
If we do, people are apt to say that we are doing all things
well. Any reasonable person will make allowances for some
mistakes. But for a bad spirit there is no acceptable alibi.

Certainly those of us who know the Master personally can
join the observers of His day and say: "He has done all things
well."

Mark 8

JESUS THE MESSIAH

8:29. "Thou art the Christ."

I. HISTORICAL SETTING. After the healing of the deaf mute in Decapolis, Jesus fed the four thousand. This second miraculous feeding is recorded only by Matthew and Mark.

Then He crossed the lake again to the west side. Here the Pharisees asked from Him a sign from heaven to prove that He was the Messiah. But Jesus refused to satisfy their unreasonable demand. Instead He once more crossed to the northeastern shore at Bethsaida. There He healed a blind man.

But again He turned northward to escape the crowds and find opportunity for teaching His disciples. His greatest concern now was preparing them to carry on when He would soon leave.

II. EXPOSITORY MEANING. Caesarea Philippi (v. 27) was so called to distinguish it from the Caesarea on the seacoast, built by Herod the Great. This one was enlarged and beautified by Philip, Herod's son, and named in honor of Tiberius Caesar. It was located at the foot of towering Mount Hermon (9,166 feet elevation). The place is called Banias today, after its ancient Greek name Pan, which means "all."

III. DOCTRINAL VALUE. This is the high point doctrinally in the Synoptic Gospels. Jesus asked His disciples for a declaration of their faith in Him, and Peter rose magnificently to the occasion. The longer form of the confession as found in Matthew 16:16 reads: "Thou art the Christ, the Son of the living God." This is the strongest affirmation of the deity of Jesus in the Synoptic Gospels.

IV. PRACTICAL AIM. To challenge our understanding of who Jesus is. Do we believe in Him by hearsay or by actual experience?

V. HOMILETICAL FORM

Theme: "Jesus the Messiah."

Introduction: The place was propitious. Called Pan by the Greeks, it was situated at the foot of majestic Mount Hermon. Here the Jordan River leaped from a rocky cleft to begin its long journey southward to the Sea of Galilee and onward to the Dead Sea.

Right here at the shrine of the ancient Greek All-God, Jesus called forth the confession of His messiahship. He, not Pan, was the divine Supreme Being.

A. *The Common Question.* "Whom do men say that I am?"

No man could have the miraculous ministry that Jesus did without causing men to ask, "Who is he?" Doubtless that question was on the lips of hundreds of people in Galilee. They had seen Him heal the sick, cast out demons, feed the multitudes. They heard that He had even raised the dead, and stilled the storm. Who could this be?

First the Master asked His disciples what men were saying about Him. They furnished a variety of opinions that were going the rounds. Some, like Herod (cf. 6:16), thought that John the Baptist had come to life again. Others, remembering that Elijah had performed miracles and that Malachi (4:5) had predicted the reappearance of the old prophet, identified Jesus with Him. Others simply said, "One of the prophets." Surprisingly, no one suggested that He might be the Messiah.

B. *The Crucial Question.* "But whom say ye that I am?"

It is important to know what others are saying about Jesus. But the crucial question is our own belief about Him.

The Greek is very emphatic: "But you (pl.), who do you say me to be?" For many months the disciples had been with Jesus. They had eaten, slept, traveled and talked with Him. They had seen Him under all sorts of conditions and circumstances. He had been equal to every occasion. Whether confronted by disease, death, demons, or the stormy deep, He had always been the mighty Conqueror. What was their conclusion concerning Him?

There is no more important question in the world than, "What think ye of Christ?" The answer to that determines our character here and our destiny hereafter.

C. *The Confident Confession.* "Thou art the Christ!"

Peter was one of the first four fishermen called to follow the Lord. He had had enough faith in Jesus to forsake his business and follow this new Leader. He had witnessed the many miracles of the Master. He was one of the inner circle of three who had seen Jairus' daughter raised from the dead. What effect had all this had on him? The answer is found in his ringing declaration: "Thou art the Christ."

"The Christ" is Greek for "the Messiah" (Hebrew). The prophets of old had foretold the coming of the Messiah, the "hope of Israel." Long centuries had waited. At last He had appeared!

It took courage for Peter to declare openly that Jesus was actually the Messiah. But his courage was born of conviction, which in turn was based on growing consciousness of a divine Presence. The only way today that we can really know that Jesus is the Christ is through personal experience of His divine Person and Power.

Mark 8

THE PATHWAY TO LIFE

8:34. "Whosoever will come after me, let him deny himself, and take up his cross, and follow me."

I. HISTORICAL SETTING. The first thing that Jesus had to do after the confession at Caesarea Philippi was to straighten out the distorted concept of the Messiah held by the Jews of His day. They looked for a coming king, a son of David who would overthrow their enemies, free them from foreign domination, and rule over Israel and the world in glory and splendor.

But first must come the Cross. So Jesus made the first prediction of the Passion (v. 31). This forms the background for His call to the disciples to accept the Cross also for themselves.

II. EXPOSITORY MEANING. "Will save" (v. 35) is not the future tense of the verb, as this tranlation might suggest. The Greek says: "Whoever wishes to save." The word "life" (twice in v. 35) is the same in the Greek (*psyche*) as "soul" in verses 36 and 37. In the King James Version it is translated "soul" 58 times, "life" 40 times, "mind" 3 times, and once each "heart" and "heartily." Twice it is left untranslated. It is of interest to note that not only the Revised Standard Version but also the Berkeley Version uses "life" throughout this passage (vv. 35-37).

III. DOCTRINAL VALUE. The main emphasis of the text is on self-renunciation as the gateway to spiritual life. That must be followed by self-crucifixion, and this in turn by a life of constant obedience. Christ took this path, and if we would follow Him we must take it too.

The value of the human soul is also underscored in the context. It is worth more than all the world. To lose it is to lose all.

IV. PRACTICAL AIM. To show that there is no easy way
to follow Jesus. It calls for the denial and death of self. It
demands full obedience. It means accepting Christ's pattern of
life as ours.

V. HOMILETICAL FORM

Theme: "The Pathway to Life."

Introduction: There are two basic philosophies of life. One
is that of Nietzsche, the German philosopher, who said, "Assert
yourself!" This helped to produce the superman, Hitler, who
drenched the world in blood. The other is that of Jesus Christ,
who said, "Deny yourself." He shed His own blood to save a
world and bring peace on earth.

A. *Denial of Self*. "Let him deny himself."

Over the doorway to the Christian life are written these
words: "Deny yourself, all ye who would enter here." Frankly,
that is why so few enter. Self-denial is the price that most people are not willing to pay. They will sacrifice money, time,
and energy. But to deny one's self — that is asking too much!

It should be noted that Jesus did not say: "Let him deny
himself of this or that." He said, "Let him deny himself"—
period! Actual denial of *self* is something far different from
popular conceptions of self-denial. The latter may mean only
sacrificing a nickel chocolate bar to give to missions. The former demands a self-renunciation that involves rejecting our
way to accept Christ's way. It means saying "No" to self and
"Yes" to Him.

B. *Death of Self*. "take up his cross."

For many people carrying one's cross means enduring some
or less inevitable affliction, such as rheumatism. But Jesus said,
"take up his cross." That indicates a voluntary acceptance of
something we could reject.

The cross is the symbol of death. It means crucifixion. The
New Testament emphasizes strongly the truth that self-crucifixion is the price of power, the secret of victory. Paul said:
"Knowing this, that our old man is crucified with him, that
the body of sin might be destroyed, that henceforth we should
not serve sin" (Rom. 6:6). And again: "I have been crucified

with Christ; and no longer do I [*ego*] live, but Christ lives in me" (Gal. 2:20, lit. trans.). The order of the Greek emphasizes vividly the fact that Christ had taken the place of the carnal ego at the center of Paul's being.

Just as Christ carried His cross and then was crucified on it, so every Christian must have his Calvary of self-crucifixion. Only then can we say with Paul: "Not I, but Christ."

C. *The Determination of Self.* "follow me."

"Deny" and "take up" are both in the aorist tense, suggesting the crises of conversion and consecration. But "follow" is in the present tense, signifying continuous action. There must be the constant determination of one's will to follow Christ fully, clear to the end. This is a lifelong assignment.

The setting of this text is very significant. Jesus had just predicted His passion. To follow Him meant to take the Calvary road. As for Him, so for all His followers there is no resurrection without a preceding crucifixion. The resurrection life of victory is possible only to those who have died with Christ.

Mark 9

THE TRANSFIGURED CHRIST

9:2. "He was transfigured before them."

I. HISTORICAL SETTING. The first verse of this chapter probably belongs with the previous chapter (cf. Matt. 16:28; 17:1). The reference could hardly be to the Transfiguration, which took place only one week later. Probably the correct interpretation is that it applies to Pentecost and its postlude — the spread of the kingdom of God in the power of the Spirit.

The "high mountain" where Jesus took the three disciples "apart by themselves" is traditionally identified with Mount Tabor, between Galilee and Samaria. But this is a rather low knoll (1000 ft). Furthermore, there are indications of a military fortress on its summit in Roman times. So most scholars today favor Mount Hermon because of its height and seclusion.

II. EXPOSITORY MEANING. "After six days" (v. 2; Matt. 17:1) is "about an eight days after" in Luke 9:28. Both expressions mean "a week later." "Tabernacles" (v. 5) probably means booths made of tree branches. The "cloud" (v. 7) suggests the Shekinah of the Old Testament. "Beloved" also carries the sense of "only." The reference in verse 13 is to John the Baptist, as Matthew (17:13) explains.

III. DOCTRINAL VALUE. This passage highlights the deity of Jesus more than almost any other in the Synoptics. We find here not only the display of His divine glory but also the definite word from heaven: "This is my beloved Son: hear him" (v. 7). The doctrine of immortality is also suggested, for Moses and Elijah are still alive.

IV. PRACTICAL AIM. To challenge us to live the transfigured life.

V. HOMILETICAL FORM

Theme: "The Transfigured Christ."

Introduction: Every great life is marked by great crises. So it was with Jesus. There was the Baptism, the Temptation, and now the Transfiguration. Most of life is lived on the plain of daily duty. But this must be punctuated at times with mountain top experiences, if life is to take on its larger meanings.

A. *The Meaning of the Transfiguration.* "after six days."

Six days after — after what? After the confession at Caesarea Philippi and the prediction of the Passion that followed. Peter had declared: "Thou art the Messiah!" To him it now seemed the time had come to set up the messianic kingdom in Jerusalem. What a day!

But suddenly everything was shattered. Jesus asserted that He was not going up to Jerusalem for a crown but for a cross, not to reign, but to die. Immediately Peter protested. This must not be. In reply Jesus rebuked the apostle, called him an adversary, and indicated he did not look at things as God does. Then He taught His disciples that they too must take the way of the Cross (8:34). All this left them sad and confused. Was He really the Christ?

The Transfiguration was the answer — at least for Peter, James, and John. They saw the inner divine glory burst through the bonds of flesh, shine through the veil, and show itself in unmistakable brilliance. They caught a glimpse of God's glory in the face of Jesus Christ. He was more than a mere man. He was truly the Son of God!

Thus all haunting fears were dispelled again by faith. The Transfiguration was a confirmation of the confession at Caesarea Phillippi.

But what about the death of their Messiah? The answer came in the conversation with Moses and Elijah (cf. Luke 9:31). It was all a part of heaven's plan for earth's salvation.

B. *The Message of the Transfiguration.* "This is my beloved Son: hear him."

Twice came this voice from heaven: at the Baptism and at the Transfiguration. It was God's exclamation point placed after Peter's confession. It was the divine attestation of the human affirmation.

The second part of the message, "hear him," was probably a rebuke to Peter's suggestion about making three booths. By implication he put Jesus on the same level with the two human prophets. But Christ is utterly unique. He stands alone as Lord of all.

C. *The Moral of the Transfiguration.* "They saw no man any more, save Jesus only with themselves."

Peter had become absorbed with vision and visitors. But all these were to disappear. What was left? Jesus only!

The value of a vision depends on the deposit that remains. That is true of all experiences of ecstasy or emotion. Do they leave us different? Do we find the presence of our Lord more real and precious because we have seen Him in a new light? That is the real test of all religious experience. Unless, at least in a measure, it transforms and transfigures us, it is not a genuine spiritual experience.

How may we live the transfigured life? By letting the divine Presence fill our hearts and flood our personalities, so as to shine out through our lives. Thus shall we re-present Christ to the world.

Mark 9

THE HIGH COST OF CARELESSNESS

9:43. "And if thy hand offend thee, cut it off."

9:45. "And if thy foot offend thee, cut it off."

9:47. "And if thine eye offend thee, pluck it out."

I. HISTORICAL SETTING. The Mount of Transfiguration was followed by the valley of trouble. Jesus could not stay on the mount of heavenly fellowship when there was dire, distressing need below. So He came and healed the boy who was demon-possessed (vv. 14-29). Then He headed down through Galilee, avoiding the crowds, for he wanted to teach His disciples. He told them a second time of His coming passion (vv. 30-32).

Finally they arrived in Capernaum. There He chided them for their dispute as to who should be the greatest (vv. 33-37). He also rebuked their narrow, sectarian spirit (vv. 38-41).

II. EXPOSITORY MEANING. The Greek verb *skandalizo* (cf. scandalize), here rendered "offend," is one of the most difficult in the New Testament to translate. According to one member of the revision committee (RSV) it was the last word on which an official vote was taken. It had baffled the committee for years. The verb comes from the noun *skandalon,* which meant the bait stick or trigger of a trap or snare. So the verb has been rendered "trap" or "ensnare." Perhaps the Revised Versions (1881, 1901) "cause to stumble" represents the meaning best.

"Millstone" (v. 42) is literally "millstone of a donkey"; that is, a large stone turned by a donkey, not one of the small, flat ones turned by women in their homes.

"Hell" is Gehenna. This is from *Ge-Hinnom,* the Valley of Hinnom south of Jerusalem. Here the Israelites offered their

children to Moloch, letting them roast to death in the arms
of his image (Jer. 7:31). King Josiah had declared the place
unclean (II Kings 23:10), and it became the city dump. The
lurid flames licking at the garbage and refuse made it a fitting
symbol of hell.

Note that "the kingdom of God" (v. 47) is equated with
(eternal) "life" (vv. 43, 45).

Verses 44 and 46 are not found in the earliest manuscripts.
Evidently they were copied in by some later scribe from verse
48, which is genuine. The "worm" speaks of gnawing memory,
one of the torments of hell.

III. DOCTRINAL VALUE. Here is to be found one of the
most definite passages on hell in the New Testament. The
nature, as well as the fact, of eternal punishment is vividly set
forth in verse 48.

IV. PRACTICAL AIM. To warn against any carelessness that
might result in being lost forever.

V. HOMILETICAL FORM
    Theme: "The High Cost of Carelessness."
    Introduction: The doctrine of hell is passé. So the sophis-
ticated say. Away with the ecclesiastical distortions that have
crept into Christianity. Give us again the simple teachings of
the gentle Jesus!

Those who talk that way have not read the Gospels carefully. Actually the strongest teaching in the New Testament
on hell as a place of eternal punishment is to be found right
here in the earliest Gospel. We cannot accept Jesus' words
about lilies and sparrows, about love and light, and reject His
plain warnings against eternal torment. They all are equally
authenticated in the sacred record.

    A. *The Offending Hand.* "If thy hand offend thee, cut it
off."

The hand is the symbol of *what we do.* If we find that some
activities are proving to be a stumbling block to us, we must
cut them off. No matter how much we enjoy doing a certain
type of thing, no matter how innocent it may seem of itself,

we must deal drastically with it. No price is too high to pay for escaping hell. That is what Jesus was saying.

Of course Christ was not advocating literal mutilation of the physical body. One cannot get rid of sin that way. He was speaking figuratively. One of the best applications of His warning is this: If you have a bosom friend, who seems as close to you as your hand, and yet he is tempting you away from God's best in your life, cut off that friendship immediately and completely! That is the only safe policy.

B. *The Offending Foot.* "If thy foot offend thee, cut it off."

The foot is the symbol of *where we go*. If you are being tempted to go places that will hurt you spiritually, do something desperate about it. A man had better change jobs or even his place of abode than to find himself lured into wrong surroundings. Whatever it is that is causing one's steps to go astray must be cut off, no matter what the cost. Any price is cheap, if it but saves us from hell. Jesus could not have put the matter more vividly and drastically.

C. *The Offending Eye.* "If thine eye offend thee, pluck it out."

The eye is the symbol of *what we see*. It is in many respects the most precious part of the body. Sooner lose a hand or a foot than one's eye.

This warning is particularly pertinent today. A generation ago those brought up in Christian homes were seldom exposed to "the lust of the eyes." But what is the situation now? Sex appeal confronting the eye almost everywhere — billboards, magazine covers at the corner drug store, theater advertising, to say nothing of the ever-present television.

What is the cure? Cut off every appeal that causes us to stumble. Sometimes this means simply shutting one's eyes to tempting sights or turning away.

Mark 10

JESUS ON DIVORCE

10:9. "What therefore God hath joined together, let not man put asunder."

I. HISTORICAL SETTING. Jesus was now on His final journey to Jerusalem, there to be crucified. For the last time He left Capernaum, which He had made His headquarters during His great Galilean ministry of perhaps a year and a half. He now went into "the coasts of Judaea by the farther side of Jordan." This was then called Perea (modern Transjordan), from *peran,* "across." Here the Pharisees came to Him with a question about divorce.

II. EXPOSITORY MEANING. "Tempting" (v. 2) is the verb *peirazo,* the primary meaning of which was "test." But it is obvious that here the Pharisees had a malicious motive. "Cleave" (v. 7) is literally "be glued to." It goes without saying that most modern marriages need more glue (unselfish love) to hold them together.

Verse 12 is not found in the parallel passage in Matthew. The latter wrote for Jews, who did not permit a woman to divorce her husband. But Mark wrote for the Romans, who gave a higher legal status to women and allowed them to divorce their husbands.

III. DOCTRINAL VALUE. The doctrine of creation is emphasized here, as well as the suggestion that man, made in the image of God, should live a godly life. It is clearly indicated that God's ideal for human marriage was monogamy.

IV. PRACTICAL AIM. To discover what Jesus had to say on the very important matter of divorce.

V. HOMILETICAL FORM
Theme: "Jesus on Divorce."
Introduction: There is hardly any other single question that

plagues modern society more than that of divorce. It confronts us on every side. Even the churches are seriously afflicted with it. What is to be done about it?

For the Christian the highest authority must always be Christ. What did He say about it? That is the most important question for us to ask. The passage before us gives the answer. Jesus did not evade this perennial problem.

A. *The Catch Question.* "Is it lawful for a man to put away his wife?"

This question is as old as time. It is not just a matter of what the law says about it. The Greek verb means, "Is it permitted? Is it proper?"

By asking this question the Pharisees hoped to get Jesus into trouble. Perea was under the rule of Herod Antipas. He had put John the Baptist to death for condemning his adulterous marriage to Herodias. If the Pharisees could trap Jesus into making some strong statement against divorce, perhaps Antipas would execute Him and they would no longer have to endure this rival. At least it was worth trying.

B. *The Counter Question.* "What did Moses command you?"

On more than one occasion Jesus met a catch question with a counter question. That is a wise way to answer those who ask "loaded" questions, seeking to get us into trouble.

The Jews held Moses as their highest authority. So this question was altogether logical and pertinent.

In reply the Pharisees answered that Moses allowed a man to write a certificate of divorce and dismiss his wife. Therefore was not divorce all right? But Jesus explained that it was because of the hardness of their hearts that Moses made this concession.

The point that should be noted is that Moses' action was intended not to encourage divorce, but to discourage it. He was seeking to make it harder, not easier. By requiring a man to engage the services of a paid scribe and set forth in writing the reasons for his action, he hoped to prevent the spread of this plague of easy divorce.

C. *The Conclusion*. "What therefore God hath joined together, let not man put asunder."

What is God's attitude toward divorce? It may be summed up in one brief statement: He is against it! As Jesus pointed out, He showed this in creation — one man, one woman. That is still God's will for humanity.

In marriage the two become "one flesh." That is why it is a sin to separate them. It is something far different from a business partnership or any other relationship of life. Not even parents and children, or brothers and sisters, sustain the close relation of husband and wife. Therefore it should be treated with utmost sacredness.

This is the basic secret of successful marriage. When it is thought of as something sacred, it can become a veritable sacrament of spiritual grace. But when lust takes the place of love, when selfishness corrodes love until it no longer deserves that name — then the marriage is headed for serious trouble.

By the very nature of marriage it is obvious that self-centered individuals clearly cannot be one in a happy union. There is no earthly relationship that more fully demands unselfish love than marriage. Only as each puts the other first can both find their highest happiness in seeking to make the other happy.

Mark 10

TRUE GREATNESS

10:45. "For even the Son of man came not to be ministered unto, but to minister, and to give his life a ransom for many."

I. HISTORICAL SETTING. After Jesus' strong statement against divorce, He blessed the little children, taking them up in His arms (vv. 13-16). Among the saddest D.P.'s of our day are the children of divorced parents. They often love both and want to live with both. But the sinful selfishness of the parents prohibits it.

Jesus was then confronted with the rich young ruler, who failed to pay the price of soul peace (vv. 17-22). For the third and last time He predicted His passion (vv. 32-34). The sordid sequel was the request of James and John that they might be first in His kingdom.

II. EXPOSITORY MEANING. The "cup" (v. 38) was a symbol of experiencing sorrow (cf. Ps. 75:8). "Baptism" was a figure for overwhelming floods of grief (cf. Isa. 43:2). It may be that the former suggests inner spiritual agony and the latter outer persecutions and afflictions. "Displeased" (v. 41) is "indignant." "Exercise lordship" (v. 42) is literally "lord it (over them)." "Minister" (v. 43) is *diakonos,* which simply means "servant." The verb (v. 45) may well be translated "not to be served, but to serve."

III. DOCTRINAL VALUE. The Greek word for "ransom" (v. 45) was used at that time for the redemption money paid for the freeing of a slave. "For" is *anti,* which in the papyri of that period most frequently means "instead of." Here it definitely supports the idea of Christ's substitutionary atonement. He not only died "for" us but in our place. He secured our release from sin by the payment of His own life's blood.

IV. PRACTICAL AIM. To see what true greatness is and also to appreciate Christ's atoning work for us.

V. HOMILETICAL FORM

Theme: "True Greatness."

Introduction: What a sorry spectacle of self-ambition! Jesus had for the third time predicted His coming suffering and death at Jerusalem. Right on the heels of that, James and John came to Him, requesting the seats of honor on either side of Him in glory. They were ready for a throne, but not for thorns. They wanted a coronation, not a crucifixion; self-indulgence, not sacrifice. How it must have hurt the heart of Jesus to see the selfishness and spiritual blindness of His disciples — yes, two who had been with Him on the Mount of Transfiguration. That vision seemed only to have whetted their anticipation of the coming kingdom. But they wanted to bypass the suffering that always must precede the glory.

A. *The Price of Greatness.* "Can ye drink of the cup that I drink of? and be baptized with the baptism that I am baptized with?"

Many people desire greatness, but few find it. The simple reason is that they are not willing to pay the price. True greatness never comes without a costly period of preparation. Only those who have experienced the discipline of suffering can develop the highest character.

When asked, "Can ye?" the disciples glibly replied, "We can." How little they understood the meaning of His words! What were they doing while He was agonizing in prayer in the Garden? Sleeping! What did they do when He was arrested? "They all forsook him and fled." Where were they when He was tried before Pilate and led away to be crucified? Missing!

But what of people today who thoughtlessly sing the song, "We are Able"? Do many, or any, really understand what they are singing. Too often it sounds like empty boasting.

B. *The Practice of Greatness.* "Whosoever will be great among you, shall be your minister [servant]."

When the other ten heard of James' and John's request they were indignant. Knowing the selfishness of their hearts we may wonder if they were jealous because they had not thought to ask first!

Jesus called them all to Him and gave them a lesson on true greatness. He reminded them of the world's way of looking at it: great men lord it over those under them. But the Master said that His men must be different. The one who would be great must be the servant of the rest, and the one who desired to be chief of all must be the slave (*doulos*) of all. This is the Christian way.

C. *The Paragon of Greatness.* "For even the Son of man came not to be ministered unto, but to minister, and to give his life a ransom for many."

The supreme example of true greatness is none other than Jesus Christ Himself. He practiced what He preached. But He went beyond anything that we can. Not only did He live a life of unselfish service, but He finally gave Himself as the supreme sacrifice for our sins.

The theological implications of this verse are tremendous. The price of our freedom from the slavery of sin was the death of Christ on the Cross. Gladly He paid the ransom, the redemption price of His own blood, that we might be released. He took our place as a condemned criminal and died in our stead. There could be no greater proof of infinite divine love.

Mark 11

THE TRIUMPHAL ENTRY

11:9. "Hosanna; Blessed is he that cometh in the name of the Lord."

I. HISTORICAL SETTING. The place was the Mount of Olives, across the Kidron Valley from Jerusalem. As the group of Galilean pilgrims came up the Jericho road and approached the village of Bethany on the east slope of the mount, Jesus sent two disciples ahead to Bethphage. He instructed them to bring a colt on which He could ride into Jerusalem. This was the first Palm Sunday at the beginning of Passion Week.

II. EXPOSITORY MEANING. The location of Bethphage is not certain. But references to it in the Talmud seem to place it on the western slope of the Mount of Olives, facing Jerusalem. Bethphage means "house of figs," Bethany "house of dates."

The Greek of verse 3 (latter part) reads thus: "Say: 'the Lord has need of it, and he is sending it immediately back here.' "

"Hosanna" (v. 9) literally means "Save now" or "Save, we pray." But here it seems to be more an exclamation of praise, like "God save the King!" Luke interprets it for his Greek readers as meaning "glory."

"Temple" (v. 11) is the Temple Area. His quick survey of conditions there was in preparation for His cleansing of the temple the next day.

III. DOCTRINAL VALUE. The striking fact is that when Jesus was acclaimed as the Messiah, He did not protest. If He was not the Christ, He was not even a good man, but a deceiver.

IV. PRACTICAL AIM. To encourage our hearts to welcome Christ as King of kings and Lord of lords in our individual lives.

V. HOMILETICAL FORM
   Theme: "The Triumphal Entry."
   Introduction: It was Jesus' last visit to Jerusalem. Frequently He had returned there for the annual festivals — Passover, Pentecost, Tabernacles — only to be criticized for His acts of mercy and to have His life threatened by the Jewish leaders. Now He would give them their last opportunity.

   A. *The Preparation.* "He sendeth forth two of his disciples."
   Jesus never did anything haphazardly or without careful preparation. It was Sunday morning and He was approaching Jerusalem at the climax of His earthly mission. Before the final rejection of the Jewish nation as the special people of God, He must offer Himself publicly as the Messiah. They must be given every opportunity to accept Him as such.

   So he sent for a colt. Zechariah had prophesied (9:9): "Behold thy King cometh unto thee: he is just, and having salvation; lowly, and riding upon an ass, and [even] upon a colt the foal of an ass." Deliberately Jesus acted out this prophecy as Himself the fulfilment of it. But even though the Jewish leaders were very familiar with this messianic passage, they refused to accept Jesus. In their minds and hearts they had already rejected Him and they stubbornly refused to change.

   B. *The Procession.* "They that went before, and they that followed."
   Though the leaders of the nation met the Master with final and full rejection, the Galilean pilgrims who had learned to love Him greeted Him with acclaim. For them it was truly a triumphal entry.

   So stirred were they that many laid their outer garments in the road as a "red carpet" for Him to ride on. Others, with more caution, spread a litter of leaves on the path. All were mightily moved with the excitement of the moment. This was the hour toward which they had looked so long. The Messiah had come! A new age had dawned!

And so it was. But not in the way they anticipated.

C. *The Praise.* "Hosanna; Blessed is he that cometh in the name of the Lord: . . . Hosanna in the highest."

This was more than welcoming some new prophet. The language of verse 10 shows that the shouting pilgrims expected the immediate setting up of the messianic kingdom. Roman rule would be ended. The Golden Age had come. It was the fulfilment of the ages.

But sin triumphed that day. The reaction of the religious leaders (cf. Matt. 21:15; Luke 19:41-44) demonstrated conclusively that what the nation, and the world, needed was not a military conqueror but a Savior from sin. There were tears in the Triumphal Entry, and it left Jesus with a sob in His soul. Only He realized the tragic price the Jews must pay for their rejection of the Messiah.

It is still costly to reject the Savior — the most costly thing that one can do. What are we doing to Jesus today?

Mark 11

THE POWER OF FAITH

11:22. "have faith in God."

I. HISTORICAL SETTING. The Triumphal Entry was on Sunday. The next morning Jesus, on His way into Jerusalem from Bethany, saw a fig tree with leaves on it. He stopped to see if it might have fruit, but it had none. So He declared it should never again bear fruit. He did not curse it for not having fruit, but for giving the impression, by its leaves, that it did. Its destruction was a significant warning of what was to happen to the Jewish nation for claiming religion but having no fruit of genuine righteousness.

That same day, Monday, Jesus cleansed the temple. A corner of the Court of the Gentiles had been turned into a cattle and sheep market, as well as a money exchange. Jesus put an end to that and forbade the use of the sacred area as a thoroughfare for those carrying burdens across the city. He accused the priests of making God's house of prayer a den of robbers.

Tuesday morning, as they once more returned to the city, Peter noted that the fig tree had already withered, and called Jesus' attention to it. From it, the Master proceeded to teach His disciples a lesson on faith.

II. EXPOSITORY MEANING. "The time of figs" (v. 13) is normally June. But this was about the first of April. "Temple" (v. 15) does not mean a building (the Sanctuary), but the Temple Area and specifically the outer, open Court of the Gentiles. The "money-changers" were there because the annual temple tax had to be paid with the Phoenician silver half shekel, worth about thirty-five cents. The money in common use was Roman. "Thieves" (v. 17) should be "robbers." Robbery is theft with force. "Doctrine" (v. 18) is simply "teaching." The imperfect tense of verse 19 probably indicates customary action: "and every evening he went forth out of the city" (ASV) .

III. DOCTRINAL VALUE. Jesus' divine power was once more displayed in causing the fig tree to wither quickly. But He intimated that any one with full faith in God could accomplish miraclous things.

IV. PRACTICAL AIM. To show the great possibilities of faith and also the necessity for faith and a spirit of forgiveness if our prayers are to be answered.

V. HOMILETICAL FORM

Theme: "The Power of Faith."

Introduction: Jesus cursed the braggart fig tree, and it withered away. This was a parable of the death of the Jewish nation because of its hypocrisy.

Between the cursing and the withering came the cleansing of the temple. Against "all the sweltering of a dirty cattle-market and the haggling of a dirtier exchange of money" Jesus revolted with all His soul. The dishonesty and greed caused Him to call the temple a den of robbers. People had to have animals for sacrifice that were approved by the priests. It was safer to buy these cattle and sheep at the temple than to run the risk of having one's own animals rejected. Also the temple tax had to be paid with Phoenician money, and the priests' representatives charged about fifteen percent for exchanging Roman money. No wonder Jesus called the place a den of robbers!

Every evening Jesus went outside the city, where He would be safer from secret assassination. The city of the Great King was no safe place for the King when He came.

A. *The Command of Faith.* "Have faith in God."

God is both the source and object of our faith. The Greek of this text says literally, "Have faith of God." This could be the possessive genitive: "Have God's faith"; that is, the faith which God gives. In Ephesians 2:8 we read that faith is the gift of God. But here more likely it is objective genitive: "Have faith in God."

Faith in anything or anyone less than God spells inevitable disappointment. All else will let us down. But He never!

B. *The Character of Faith.* "shall not doubt in his heart."

Faith is a firm conviction that what God has promised He will do. Ultimately it is trust in a Person — the all-wise, all-powerful, all-loving Heavenly Father.

Jesus said that if one commanded a mountain to be cast into the sea, and did not doubt in his heart, it would be done. Of course He was not talking about the Mount of Olives, as some have said. God does not busy Himself doing silly, unnecessary things. "Removing mountains" was a Jewish figure of speech for getting rid of a great difficulty. The disciples would understand what the Master meant. Christians are still seeing impossible barriers moved out of the way in answer to believing prayer.

But faith must be constant. "Believe" (v. 24) is literally "keep on believing." That is one of the main requirements for answered prayer. Too often we get discouraged and quit believing before the fulfilment of our petition.

C. *The Condition of Faith.* "Forgive."

Faith without forgiveness is impossible. The reason some people cannot believe is their wrong attitude. If we have an unforgiving spirit toward anyone it effectually blocks our prayers and destroys our faith. Faith will not operate in the atmosphere of unforgiveness.

The first requirement for successful praying is utter sincerity of soul. We must bare our hearts before God if we expect Him to hear and answer our prayers.

Mark 11

SHOULD WE PAY TAXES?

12:17. "Render to Caesar the things that are Caesar's, and to God the things that are God's."

I. HISTORICAL SETTING. After Jesus gave the lesson of faith, based on the barren fig tree, He once more entered Jerusalem. Here He was confronted by members of the Sanhedrin, who demanded to know on whose authority He had cleansed the temple. In turn Jesus asked them a question: Was John the Baptist's authority divine or human? The disgraceful ethical attitude of these religious leaders is laid bare in verses 31 and 32. They were governed by expediency rather than moral righteousness. Christ was altogether justified in asking what He did, for the correct answer to His question would be the answer to theirs.

Then Jesus told the parable of the wicked husbandman. The leaders recognized that they were the villains of the parable and wanted to kill Jesus. But they were afraid of the people. So they bided their time.

II. EXPOSITORY MEANING. The Herodians are not mentioned by Josephus. But their name indicates that they were supporters of the Roman rule of the Herods. The Greek word for "catch" (v. 13) means to "catch" or "take" by hunting or fishing. "In his words" is "by a word" or "in a statement." The "tribute" (v. 14) was the poll tax. The "penny" was a denarius, worth about twenty cents.

III. DOCTRINAL VALUE. Jesus' teaching included man's civic and social, as well as spiritual, responsibilities. On the subject of paying taxes compare Romans 13:7; I Peter 2:13f.

IV. PRACTICAL AIM. To show that one should fulfill his lawful obligations to the government and also to God.

V. HOMILETICAL FORM

Theme: "Should We Pay Taxes?"

Introduction: The Pharisees and the Herodians were sworn enemies. The former were the nationalists, who hated foreign rule. The latter were politicians who supported it. But they got together in their common enmity for Christ. Men still do that today.

A. *The Question.* "Is it lawful to give tribute to Caesar, or not?"

Note the "softening" process. They tried to flatter Jesus by saying they knew He did not care what anybody thought about His teaching; He told the truth always, fearless of the consequences. They thus hoped to put Him off His guard, so that He might carelessly make a statement that would get Him into trouble. Then they popped their question: "Is it lawful to pay a poll tax to Caesar or not?

They thought they had Him caught on either horn of the dilemma, so that He could not escape. If He said "Yes" the Pharisees would tell the people that He was unpatriotic, a traitor to the nation. But if He said "No" the Herodians would promptly report Him to the authorities as a dangerous revolutionary who was teaching the people not to pay their poll tax as an acknowledgment of Roman rule. It would be impossible for this upstart prophet to escape now!

B. *The Request.* "Bring me a penny."

The Jewish leaders had not reckoned with Jesus' insight into their character. He saw right through their hypocrisy. Instead of answering their question He asked for a denarius. Looking at it He asked whose picture was on it. It was a bust of Tiberius Caesar, the reigning emperor at Rome. On the other side of the coin was his inscription.

C. *The Command.* "Render to Caesar the things that are Caesar's and to God the things that are God's."

Jesus' logic was incisive, inescapable: "Well, if this coin carries Caesar's image and superscription, it looks to me as if it belongs to him; so you had better give it back to him." He might have implied: "Why are you carrying Caesar's picture around in your pocket if you hate him so?"

Jesus made himself perfectly clear on the subject of paying taxes. He taught that taxes are a debt we owe the government for services rendered. The verb "render" is literally "give back." We do not *give* taxes or tithe; we *pay* them. They are an obligation which it is our responsibility to meet.

Jesus did not stop with answering their question. As often, He went the second mile and gave more than was asked. Here He added: "and to God the things that are God's."

What are the things that are God's? Primarily the soul. For it bears on it, though marred, the image and superscription of its Creator. But the statement is all-inclusive. Everything we have comes ultimately from God and should be held at His disposal. It is really His. We are just the stewards of His property. Christian stewardship demands a complete consecration to God of all our time and talent, our strength and energy.

Mark 12

THE PRIMACY OF LOVE

12:30. "Thou shalt love the Lord thy God with all thy heart, and with all thy soul, and with all thy mind, and with all thy strength."

12:31. "Thou shalt love thy neighbor as thyself."

I. HISTORICAL SETTING. After the Pharisees and Herodians asked their question about paying taxes, the Sadducees had their try. Since they did not believe in any resurrection, they presented the hypothetical case of a woman who had seven husbands. Which one would claim her at the resurrection? They hoped to show how absurd this doctrine of the Pharisees (and Jesus) was. But Christ charged them with error due to not knowing the Scriptures or the power of God and proceeded to prove that the resurrection is implied in the Pentateuch, the only Scripture accepted by the Sadducees.

II. EXPOSITORY MEANING. The "scribes" (v. 28) were mostly Pharisees, who believed in the resurrection. One of them, pleased that Jesus had so effectually answered the Sadducees, asked a point of information. Literally the question reads: "Of what kind is the principal commandment of all?" That is, the scribe wished to know what was of highest importance in religion. The Rabbis had divided the 613 precepts of the Law (248 commands and 365 prohibitions) into "weighty" and "light." The scribe wanted to know which was most weighty.

In reply Jesus referred him to the Shema (Deut. 6:4, 5), which every pious Pharisee repeated twice a day. This was the most significant single Scripture passage in the eyes of the Pharisees, and the scribe expressed his approval of Jesus' answer (vv. 32, 33).

III. DOCTRINAL VALUE. Three doctrines are here set forth. The first is the unity of God. The second is the supreme love for God which is the duty of every man made in the image of God. The third is love for one's fellowmen, which is both the result of divine love in our hearts and the demonstration of it.

IV. PRACTICAL AIM. To show the supremacy of love. Also the importance of love for others as a proof of our love for God. This love for one's fellowmen should be shown in the daily life.

V. HOMILETICAL FORM

Theme: "The Primacy of Love."

Introduction: What is the most important thing in religion? That was the question with which a scribe one day confronted Jesus. The Master's answer can be summed up in one word: *love*. That is the heart of religion.

A. *The Basis of the Divine Commandment.* "The Lord our God is one Lord."

The ground of God's authority over man is here stated briefly but clearly. If there are many gods, why should Jehovah alone be obeyed? The answer is that there is only one true God, the Jehovah of Israel. Literally the statement reads: "The Lord (Jehovah) our God, the Lord is one." Explicitly this asserts the unity of God. Implicitly it affirms His aloneness, as well as His oneness. Israel's great contribution to a world plagued with polytheism was its central emphasis on monotheism. By this is meant not only that Jehovah is the *one* God for Israel (henotheism) but that He is the *only* God who exists (monotheism). Christianity carries on this testimony to the uniqueness of the one true God.

Since Jehovah is the Creator and Lord of the universe He has a right to command our love and obedience. This is the basis of all divine law.

B. *The First Commandment.* "Thou shalt love the Lord thy God with all thy heart, and with all thy soul, and with all thy mind, and with all thy strength." The Hebrew text of the Old Testament says: heart, soul, and might. But the Septuagint (Greek translation of O.T.) has: mind, soul, and might. Jesus combined these in naming the four terms.

It is almost impossible to distinguish "heart" and "soul." Furthermore, the Hebrew word for "heart" sometimes means "understanding." The distinction between these is not the most important point here. Rather, it is recognizing that the meaning is: You are to love God with your whole being, with all your faculties. Emotion, intellect and will are all to be centered in Him. Religion must be a matter of the whole man. What God desires is the complete response of our total being.

C. *The Second Commandment.* "Thou shalt love thy neighbor as thyself."

So far as is known Jesus was the first to combine these two commandments of love to God and love to one's neighbor (Deut. 6:5 and Lev. 19:18). Mystics often emphasize only the first, and too many evangelicals have fallen into this same trap. Social gospelers tend to talk only of the second. But true religion recognizes the supreme importance of both.

There is no use for one to profess love to God if he shows no love to his neighbor (I John 4:20). The only proof one can give that he really loves God is by showing it in love to others. Furthermore, His love is "perfected" (completed) in us only as we let it flow through us in love to those about us (I John 4:12). Love unexpressed is no love at all. Love cannot exist in a vacuum. It is not something abstract. Only love concretely manifested in kindness to our fellowmen is actual love. Too many Christians have missed this truth.

Mark 13

THE WHOLE GOSPEL
FOR THE WHOLE WORLD

13:10. "And the gospel must first be published among all nations."

I. HISTORICAL BACKGROUND. After the three questions that Jesus had been asked — by the Pharisees and Herodians, by the Sadducees, and by a scribe — He posed one of His own: How can the Messiah be both David's Lord and David's son? No reply was offered. But the incarnation gives the answer: Jesus Christ was both God and man, both David's Lord and his descendant.

The incident of the widow's mite followed. Jesus declared that giving is not measured by the amount given but by the amount left over. The widow gave most because she gave all.

As Jesus left the temple, where He had been teaching, His disciples called attention to its massive stones and magnificent buildings. In reply He made the startling prediction that all of this would be destroyed. A little later, as He was sitting on the Mount of Olives opposite the temple the four fisherman disciples asked Him when all this was to happen. Christ's extended answer is called the Olivet Discourse, because it was given on the Mount of Olives.

II. EXPOSITORY MEANING. Mark gives the question of the disciples as twofold: "When shall these things be? and what shall be the sign when all these things shall be fulfilled?" (v. 4). Matthew makes it threefold: "When shall these things be? and what shall be the sign of thy coming, and of the end of the world?" (Matt. 24:3).

The exposition of the Olivet Discourse is not easy. Rather clearly some elements in it refer to the destruction of Jerusalem and of the temple, which took place 40 years later (A.D.

70). Just as clearly some things can be taken only as predicting events still future now, connected with the Second Coming and the close of this age. But how to separate these items is the problem.

Probably the best solution lies in the recognition of the telescopic principle of prophecy. There is a nearer, partial fulfilment in the time of the prophet. But there is also a distant complete fulfilment in Christ, in connection with either His first or His second coming. To fail to recognize this is to become entangled in hopeless confusion. Incidentally this is the solution to the much debated problem of Isaiah 7:14.

III. DOCTRINAL VALUE. The doctrine of the Second Coming bulks large in the New Testament. Hence we have no right to ignore it today. Although eschatology has been an open field for all kinds of wild speculation, it is an important part of Biblical theology. What is needed is sane and sensible handling of the subject.

IV. PRACTICAL AIM. To show how we may hasten the coming of Christ, and show what our responsibility is in the matter.

V. HOMILETICAL FORM
Theme: "The Whole Gospel for the Whole World."
Introduction: The Olivet Discourse is the only lengthy message of Jesus which is recorded in all three Synoptic Gospels. Hence its importance should not be overlooked. It is significant that the longest common discourse should be on the Second Coming.

Just because many people have gone "off the deep end" in foolish speculation on this subject — setting dates and trying to identify the Antichrist — is no excuse for our neglect of this important Biblical theme. Rather we should seek to discover our responsibility. Can we do anything to help bring an end to the rising tide of wickedness? Our text gives the answer.

A. *The Gospel.* Missions is more than a matter of medicine or education, important as these are. It is fundamentally the giving of the gospel.

What is the gospel? It is the good news that Jesus Christ came into the world to save sinners. It begins with the recognition of human sin, but goes on to the proclamation of a divine Savior. Only a whole gospel can save a lost sinner.

B. *The Giving*. A gospel that is not given benefits no one. A truth that is kept to ourselves saves no sinner. It is only the gospel *preached* which is the power of God unto salvation to everyone that believeth. How shall they call upon Him of whom they have not heard? How shall they hear without a preacher? Those are still crucial questions.

To be responsible for souls being forever lost? To enjoy the gospel but fail to share it? Are we guilty?

C. *The Going*. Giving the gospel to the whole world means that someone must go. In fact it means that all Christians must go, at least by money and prayers.

Jesus declared that the gospel must first be published to all nations. Matthew (24:14) adds: "and then shall the end come." The end of what? The end of this age. The end of the horrible reign of wickedness. Only the coming of Christ in power and glory (v. 26) will bring an end to sin and the beginning of His reign of righteousness.

For this all Christians devoutly pray. But can we do anything about it? A familiar Scripture speaks of "Looking for and hasting unto the coming of the day of God" (II Peter 3:12). But a more accurate rendering is "expecting and speeding" the day of God. That is, by our work we are to hasten the coming of Christ!

This supplements what Jesus said. When will He return? When the gospel has been preached to all nations. Has that happened? Nearly so. Not every individual, not every tribe has heard the Word of God. But is there any "nation" that has not been reached at all?

Our responsibility is to see that this task of world evangelization is completed. With the modern means of communication and transportation the job can be done. It must be done! We should not pray for Christ to come unless we are willing to help answer our prayers.

Mark 13

THE MASTER'S RETURN

13:33. "Take ye heed, watch and pray: for ye know not when the time is."

I. HISTORICAL SETTING. This is the same as for the last text. Jesus probably uttered these words in A.D. 30, a few days before His death. Forty years later, in A.D. 70, they found a partial fulfilment in the destruction of Jerusalem. In the final war (A.D. 66-70) the Christians in Jerusalem remembered the warning of Jesus and fled from the city, finding a safe refuge at Pella, east of the Jordan River. Thus they escaped the awful horrors of the last months of the siege, as well as the death or slavery that followed. This was the worst "affliction" that had ever overtaken the Jews (v. 19) because they unjustifiably expected supernatural deliverance which did not come. The mental and spiritual anguish aggravated the physical torture of those days.

II. EXPOSITORY MEANING. It would seem that the Olivet Discourse may be divided into three sections. The first (vv. 5-13) is perhaps a general introduction, dealing with both A.D. 70 and the end of the age. The second (vv. 14-23) deals primarily with the former event, while the third (vv. 24-37) relates to the latter. This division will give some guidance in the interpretation.

"Sorrows" (v. 8) is literally "birth-pangs." The troubles at the end of this era will be the birth pains of the Messianic Age. In a more limited way the troubles of the first century could be described in the same way.

Whether the language of verses 24 and 25 should be taken literally or figuratively has been much debated. In favor of the latter interpretation is the general nature of apocalyptic language as highly symbolical. But in our atomic space age we are faced with the evidence that these signs might be more literally fulfilled in physical creation than had ever been deemed possible.

The statement of verse 30 is admittedly difficult. If taken as referring to A.D. 70 there is no problem, of course. But we have suggested a reference to the Second Coming in this last section (vv. 24-37). Some would translate "generation" as "race." Others suggest that the generation which saw the beginning of sorrows would also see their end; that is, the events predicted for the close of this age will all take place within the period of a generation. No final solution of this question has been reached.

III. DOCTRINAL VALUE. Again, the Second Coming. Also verse 32 relates to the doctrine of the Kenosis. What self-limitations of knowledge or power did the Son of God impose upon himself in the Incarnation? That is an important question, but one not easy to answer.

IV. PRACTICAL AIM. In the last text we noted the responsibility of the church to hasten the return of Christ by evangelizing the world. In this text we see the challenge to personal preparedness by watching and praying.

V. HOMILETICAL FORM
    Theme: "The Master's Return.

Introduction: The subject of the Second Coming is one from which the majority of Christendom has shied away. This is understandably due to the fanatical extremes of foolish exposition often associated with it. But there is far too much on this theme in the New Testament — Gospels, Epistles, and Revelation alike — for us to pass it by. The careful reader of God's Word will realize that there are few things more important for us as individual Christians than to be ready for our Lord's return.

    A. *When?* "Of that day and that hour knoweth no man."

Seldom has more breath and ink been wasted on any subject than on the time of Christ's coming again. This is all the more amazing in the light of Jesus' careful, repeated warning that no one knows the day or the hour. Some have gone so far as to affirm: "Yes, but He did not say we could not know the year." That kind of exegesis leads only into the quagmire of senseless confusion.

Jesus said that even He himself did not know. Only the Father had the schedule. How silly, then, for men to claim more knowledge than Christ by setting dates. But this plague has afflicted the church from early days.

B. *Watch*. "Take ye heed, watch and pray."

Not "when?" but "watch!" That is the emphasis in Jesus' teaching about the Second Coming. It is also Paul's and Peter's and John's. It should be ours.

It is a sad thing that some who have speculated about the date of Christ's return have failed to be prepared for it. Their contentious, dogmatic spirit shows an un-Christlike character that has no place in the kingdom of God.

Our most important concern personally should be to keep our hearts in tune with heaven. This can come about only as we fellowship with our tarrying Lord, as we "pray" with a sense of His presence with us. If there is unbroken, unhindered communion with Christ, we have the assurance that we are ready for His return.

The word "watch" in verse 33 means "do not be sleeping"; that is, "keep awake." A different verb for "watch" is used in verses 35 and 37, but with essentially the same emphasis; namely, "be watchful." Taken together the threefold warning means: "Keep awake; be always on the alert." That is Christ's closing word in this great discourse.

C. *Why?* "For ye know not when the time is."

If the watchman knew when the thief was coming, he would be prepared at that time. Not knowing, he must be prepared all the time.

Thus it is with us. We need to maintain a continuous watch, be on the alert constantly. Only thus shall we be ready when the Master returns at that unexpected hour.

Mark 14

GETHSEMANE

14:36. "Abba, Father, all things are possible unto thee; take away this cup from me: nevertheless not what I will, but what thou wilt."

I. HISTORICAL SETTING. Apparently the Olivet Discourse was given on Tuesday afternoon. Thursday evening Jesus with His disciples celebrated the last passover (vv. 12-21) and instituted the Lord's Supper (vv. 22-25). This took place in an upper room in Jerusalem (v. 15).

After the supper they sang a hymn (v. 26). This was probably the last part of the Great Hallel ("praise"), which consisted of Psalms 115-118. Then they left for the Mount of Olives. On the way Jesus predicted that Peter would deny Him (vv. 27-31).

II. EXPOSITORY MEANING. Gethsemane (v. 32) means "oil-press," a place where oil was squeezed out of olives. This was appropriate at the foot of the Mount of the Olive Trees. Evidently Jesus entered an olive grove. "Place" in the Greek suggests a small enclosure.

"Sore amazed" (v. 33) is a rare, strong compound verb in the Greek, suggesting "terrified surprise." The same can be said for "very heavy," which means "be in anguish" or "distressed." These, with verse 34, give us just a little glimpse into the agony of "the hour" (v. 35). "Fell" is literally "was falling" (imperfect tense). It suggests the picture of Jesus staggering and stumbling until He finally fell on His face on the ground, crushed by the burden of His heart. "Abba" (v. 36) is the Aramaic word for "father." "One hour" (v. 37) may suggest the length of Jesus' first prayer. "Flesh" (v. 38) probably means the physical body. "Words" (v. 39) is singular in the Greek. The meaning is: "uttering the same petition."

The apparent conflict between verses 41 and 42 may be resolved in either of two ways. Some would make Jesus' words ironical: "Sleep then, since it is your will to do so; rest if you can." But the atmosphere of agony seems to preclude irony. The best solution is to take the words as a question: "Are you still sleeping and taking your rest?" The Greek can with equal accuracy be translated that way, and this fits the situation perfectly.

III. DOCTRINAL VALUE. The subordination of the Son to the Father is central here. Also the meaning of Christ's passion.

IV. PRACTICAL AIM. To note Christ's complete submission to the Father, as an example for us. Also to face the question: are we failing to share His sufferings?

V. HOMILETICAL FORM
  Theme: "Gethsemane."
Introduction: Christ had His Gethsemane. If we would follow Him we must also pass through the Garden — the place of full submission to the will of God.

  A. *The Sorrowing Christ.* "Take away this cup from me." The picture of Jesus' sorrow is described with startling vividness. Leaving eight disciples at the gate of the garden, He took Peter, James, and John with Him into the olive grove. Terrified surprise and extreme anguish of soul seized Him, as the black shadow of the Cross came over His consciousness. In deep distress He said to the three: "My soul is exceeding sorrowful unto death." In other words, My sorrow is killing me, is crushing the life out of me! Asking them to watch and pray, He moved a little farther into the depths of the grove. There He "was falling" on the ground, crushed to the earth by the unbearable burden of a world's sin.

What was the "cup" from which He begged to be delivered? Scoffers have called Jesus a coward. They have accused Him of cringing before the cross, of shrinking from death. But His was no martyr's fate. It was not the physical pain He dreaded. It was that moment of separation from His Father's face, when

He who knew no sin would be made sin for us. This was the deepest sorrow of Jesus' soul.

B. *The Submitting Christ.* "Nevertheless not what I will, but what thou wilt."

This was the time when Jesus deliberately took up His cross, in order to pay redemption's price. The battle was fought now, not the next day. Then He simply carried through what He had already accepted as the Father's will.

The highest prayer that any Christian can pray is: "Not my will, but thine, be done." This involves a crucial self-surrender and also a continuous self-submission. God demands of all of us nothing more and nothing less than a complete consecration to His will. That is the cost of being a Christian.

C. *The Sleeping Disciples.* "He found them asleep."

Imagine the pain and disappointment of finding the three sentries sleeping soundly at their post. But the General did not court-martial them. Reproachfully He said to Peter: "Simon, are you asleep?" This was the first time he had been addressed by that name since he was chosen as an apostle (3:16). He was not now Peter, the stone. Then to all three He said: "Watch ye and pray, lest ye enter into temptation." That is still a salutary word of warning.

Three times Jesus agonized alone in prayer. Three times He returned to the supposed prayer-partners, only to find them sound asleep. How that must have added to the sorrow of His soul.

But do we do any better than they? How often have we failed Christ in the hours of His grief over men's sins today? "If we suffer, we shall also reign with him" (II Tim. 2:12).

Mark 14

THE BIG FISHERMAN'S WORST HOUR

14:72. "When he thought thereon, he wept."

I. HISTORICAL BACKGROUND. At the close of Jesus' prayer in Gethsemane He was arrested and forsaken by all His disciples (vv. 43-52). His captors took Him to the house of the high priest, where an informal meeting of the Sanhedrin condemned Him to death (vv. 53-65). In connection with that came Peter's denial of his Lord.

II. EXPOSITORY MEANING. "The chief priests and the elders and the scribes" (v. 53) comprised the Sanhedrin, or "council" (*synedrion*, v. 55). "The Blessed" (v. 61) was a euphemism the Jews employed for God, as also "power" (v. 62). The language of verse 62 is a combination of Daniel 7:13 and Psalm 110:1.

"Palace" (v. 66) should be "courtyard." The homes of the wealthy were built around a central, open court. In the middle of this the soldiers had lighted a fire, since the spring nights are cold in the mountainous height where Jerusalem is located. The "porch" (v. 68) was the "vestibule" between the inner court and the outer door opening on the street. Peter tried to get away from the light of the fire. But his Galilean accent had given him away (v. 70).

"To curse and to swear" (v. 71) does not mean that Peter used profanity, although he may have lapsed into the rough language of a fisherman. The first verb (*anathematizo*) is used elsewhere in the New Testament only in Acts 23:12, 14, 21, where it is correctly translated "bound under a curse," and "bound with an oath." The second verb means to swear an oath, as one does in court. So what Peter was saying was this: "Let me be subject to a curse if I am not telling you the truth.

I solemnly swear under oath that I do not know this man."
This, of course, was perjury.

III. DOCTRINAL VALUE. Here, certainly, was a demonstration of the depravity of the human heart. Peter had spent
three years with Jesus. He loved his Lord. Yet disgracefully he
denied that he had ever known Him.

IV. PRACTICAL AIM. To show the danger of over-confi-
dence, of a misplaced trust in ourselves. In themselves, strong
men are weak. Also to show the forgiving grace of God for one
who fails miserably.

V. HOMILETICAL FORM
   Theme: "The Big Fisherman's Worst Hour."
   Introduction: Everyone has played the part of Peter in the
great drama of life. Sometime, somewhere, each of us has
denied his Lord.
   But the crucial question is: Have we followed Peter's role
to the finish? Have we repented with bitter tears? Have we
been forgiven and restored? Have we been called and commissioned? Have we been empowered by the Spirit? Have we,
who failed in the past, found a fruitful ministry of blessing
to humanity?
   A. *Peter's Mistakes.* "Warming himself."
   Peter made three serious mistakes which paved the path to
failure.
   1. *He disregarded warning.* Jesus said: "Verily I say unto
thee . . . thou shalt deny me thrice" (v. 30). Peter thought he
knew better than his Lord. He replied vehemently: "If I should
die with thee, I will not deny thee in any wise" (v. 31). And
he meant it. When the mob (v. 43) seized Jesus, Peter quickly
unsheathed his sword and swung at one of the servants. He
would probably have gone down fighting with his last breath
had not the Master commanded him to put away his sword.
   2. *He followed afar off* (v. 54). He wanted to play it safe.
But he got into trouble. Marginal living is actually dangerous
living.
   3. *He sat down with the wrong crowd.* It was when the
high priest's maid saw Peter "warming himself" (v. 67) with

the soldiers that she challenged him. The person who goes with wrong companions makes it easy for him to deny his Lord.

B. *Peter's Denials.* "I know not this man."

All four Gospels say that Peter was first questioned by a maid. In the garden he was a brave warrior. He was ready to defend his Master against unnumbered foes. But he wilted before the accusing finger of a maid. It is sometimes harder to meet the small things in life than the large ones.

There followed a confusion of several people confronting Peter with the charge that he was "one of them" (v. 69). This confusion is reflected in the differing accounts in the four Gospels.

Finally those standing by joined in a general accusation, based on Peter's Galilean accent. This time he declared under oath, invoking a curse on himself if he were not telling the truth, that he did not know the man they were talking about.

C. *Peter's Repentance.* "When he thought thereon, he wept."

The cock crew. Jesus turned and looked at Peter (Luke 22:61). The apostle flung himself out of the company and burst into bitter tears of repentance. Under pressure he had done what he never dreamed he would do: denied His Lord. But immediately he felt a godly sorrow which issued in genuine repentance. Peter was restored to fellowship with his Lord on the day of the Resurrection, later commissioned to feed Christ's flock, empowered by the Holy Spirit at Pentecost, and then became the foremost leader in the earliest days of the church.

Are we guilty of denying our Lord? Some do it directly, as did Peter. Others do it negatively, by failing to take their stand for Christ. Many more professing Christians deny their Christ by the way they live. Worldly, selfish, or un-Christlike living denies one's Lord. But still there is forgiveness for the repentant soul.

Mark 15

BARABBAS OR JESUS?

15:15. "And so Pilate, willing to content the people, released Barabbas unto them, and delivered Jesus, when he had scourged him, to be crucified."

I. HISTORICAL SETTING. The Jewish Sanhedrin was supposed to act with utmost justice. Its regulations required that while a verdict of acquittal could be given on the same day, a verdict of guilty must be postponed until the next day; that no criminal trial should be held at night; and that the judges who condemned a man to death must fast all day. Apparently all these rules were broken in the case of Jesus, making His trial illegal. But the Sanhedrin did hold a brief session at daybreak (v. 1), to make its sentence of condemnation official.

Then Christ was taken to Pilate. Here He maintained a poised silence, which made the governor marvel (v. 5). As Luke and John report more definitely, Pilate was convinced of Christ's innocence. Here it is noted that the governor recognized the real reason for Jesus' condemnation by the Jewish leaders (v. 10). So he sought to gain His release by way of a custom at the feast (v. 6). It did not work.

II. EXPOSITORY MEANING. Barabbas is an Aramaic name composed of *bar,* "son," and *abba,* "father"; so it means "son of the (a) father." The "insurrection" (v. 7) would be a revolt against the Roman government. This was the most serious crime in the eyes of the ruling officials. Rome was tolerant toward many things, but not when there was any threat to its authority.

It is noticeable that the chief priests took the lead in demanding Jesus' death (v. 11). Earlier, in Galilee, it had been the Pharisees who opposed Christ. But when Jesus cleansed the temple He touched both the authority and the income of the priestly Sadducees. Now they were determined to get rid of Him.

III. DOCTRINAL VALUE. The nature of sin shows up sharply here. The thin veneer of outward righteousness covered an inner rottenness. The depravity of the human heart is revealed in the way the people joined in the cry for the execution of an innocent man.

IV. PRACTICAL AIM. To understore the choice every man must make for or against Christ.

V. HOMILETICAL FORM
Theme: "Barabbas or Jesus?"
Introduction: Everyone has to make the supreme choice of his life — for or against Jesus Christ. About a thousand and one other things we can remain neutral or indifferent. But Christ confronts every man at the crossroads of life and demands a decision. Either we follow Him along the path that leads to eternal blessing or we turn our backs on Him and walk away from the Light of the world into a darkness made deeper by our own disobedience.

A. *False Son of the Father.* "released Barabbas unto them."
By a strange coincidence the name Barabbas means "son of the father." As leader of a revolt against the Roman government he posed as the savior of Israel. If the people would follow him, he would free them from foreign domination. He promised them political liberty.

This was what the people wanted. "And so Pilate, willing to content the people, released Barabbas unto them." They preferred to have a murderer loose in their midst than the Savior of mankind.

B. *True Son of the Father.* "and delivered Jesus, when he had scourged him, to be crucified."
Here was the true Son of the true Father, who had come to show the way to heaven. Far from being a murderer, He was the Giver of life. He never hurt or harmed anyone. Instead He healed and helped all those in need. What a contrast! Yet they clamored for His death.

C. *False and True Salvation*. The salvation the Jews wanted
was deliverance from foreign domination. What they failed to
realize was that the dominion of sin was a far worse calamity.
They wanted material prosperity, but ignored their deep
spiritual need.

When we view the Jewish choice of Barabbas rather than
Jesus we say, "How could they be so foolish?" Yet millions
of men still make that same choice. They prefer to hold on to
the murderer, Sin, rather than accept the Savior, Jesus. They
will follow a political or social savior who offers them economic security and political freedom, but reject the gospel of
spiritual salvation.

Never were the lines more sharply drawn than right now.
On the international level it is Communism versus Christ. On
the national scene it is materialism versus righteousness. In
each individual heart it is sin or the Savior. Barabbas or
Jesus? That is the ultimate choice every man must make.

Mark 15

SAVING ONESELF OR SAVING OTHERS

15:31 "He saved others; himself he cannot save."

I. HISTORICAL SETTING. Instead of taking Christ immediately to the place of execution the cruel Roman soldiers first staged a mock coronation. Calling the whole cohort together, they put a purple robe on Jesus. On His head they placed a crown of thorns. Then they bowed on their knees before Him in mock worship and saluted Him: "Hail, King of the Jews!" Not content with that, they smote His head with a reed and spat in His face. Quite a different coronation from what the disciples anticipated in Jerusalem!

Finally they brought Him outside the city, impressing an African, Simon, into service to carry His cross. Apparently Jesus was now too weak to carry it. At Golgotha, the place of a skull, they nailed Him to a wooden cross. The crucifixion took place at nine o'clock, and Jesus was hanging there for six hours before He died at three in the afternoon. During that period the passersby mocked Him.

II. EXPOSITORY MEANING. "Golgotha" (v. 22) is the Aramaic word for skull. The Greek word is *kranion,* from which comes the English "cranium." The familiar term "Calvary" is from the Latin *calvarium,* meaning "skull." This may have been a skull-shaped hill north of Jerusalem. We cannot be sure of the location.

They "tried to give wine mingled with myrrh" (v. 23) — this is what the imperfect tense means. But he refused to take this drug that the women of Jerusalem kindly provided for crucified criminals. It was intended to deaden the pain, but He wanted to be fully conscious.

The "third hour" was 9:00 A.M. "Thieves" (v. 27) should be "robbers." The "sixth hour" (v. 33) was noon. The "ninth

113

hour" (v. 34) was 3:00 P.M. The cry of dereliction (v. 34) was in Aramaic. "Vinegar" (v. 36) is "sour wine." The "veil" (v. 38) was the inner veil before the Holy of Holies.

III. DOCTRINAL VALUE. The whole doctrine of the Atonement is wrapped up in this incident. It cost Jesus His life to act as Mediator between a holy God and sinful men. The combination (or better, union) of the divine and the human bulks large here.

IV. PRACTICAL AIM. To note why Jesus could not save himself and at the same time save others, and its application to us.

V. HOMILETICAL FORM
    Theme: "Saving Oneself or Saving Others."
    Introduction: It was bad enough to have the soldiers mock Jesus in Pilate's Praetorium. It was worse to have the Jews who passed by rail on Him, taunting Him with His declaration that He would rebuild the temple in three days, and shouting: "Save thyself, and come down from the cross."
    But what are we to say of the chief priests, the supposedly holy attendants in the sacred sanctuary? Surely they would treat Him with respect, if not with reverence. But no, they mockingly remarked to each other: "He saved others; himself he cannot save."

    A. *The Jews Who Saved Themselves.* "Save thyself."
    This was their philosophy of life. Look out for yourself, for nobody else will. They were always thinking of their own selfish interests. Over and over again in the Gospels we see evidence of this. Self was number one in their eyes.

    B. *The Jesus Who Saved Others.* "He saved others."
    Never had the Jewish leaders spoken truer words. They may have meant them sarcastically. But they were literally and abundantly true of His whole life. He spent the days of His public ministry healing the sick, making the lame walk, strengthening the paralytics, giving sight to the blind, hearing to the deaf, and feeding the hungry. Yes, He even raised the dead. Always He was saving others.

If we would follow Jesus we must live to save others as He did. That calls for a love that manifests itself all the way from little deeds of kindness — giving a cup of cold water in His name — to intercessory prayer for lost souls. For the minister it means preaching, praying, pleading, personal work — anything to save those lost in sin. If we are not saving others, we are not following the Christ whose name we bear.

C. *The Cost of Saving Others.* "Himself he cannot save."

Saving others is expensive business. For Jesus it meant not only a life of healing ministry, involving arduous toil, but also a cruel death on a cross. There was no other way.

When the Jewish leaders mockingly said, "He saved others; himself he cannot save," they spoke better than they knew. The exact truth was that he could *not* save himself and save others. Only by losing His own life could He save others' lives.

What was true of the Master must be true of His servants. If our first concern is to save ourselves, we cannot save those around us. Selfish service will save no one. Only a sacrificial ministry can be a saving ministry. By losing ourselves in loving service for our fellowmen we shall both find a larger life and lead others to Christ.

Mark 16

THE MESSAGE OF THE EMPTY TOMB

16:6. "ye seek Jesus of Nazareth, which was crucified: he is risen; he is not here: behold the place where they laid him."

I. HISTORICAL SETTING. Friday evening before sunset, when the Sabbath Day would begin, Joseph of Arimathaea went to Pilate and boldly asked for the body of Jesus. The governor was surprised that Christ was already dead, for criminals often hung for days on the cross before finally expiring.

Joseph buried Jesus' body in a new tomb hewn out of solid rock. Two Marys watched carefully where He was laid away. On Saturday evening, when the Sabbath had ended, they brought aromatic spices for anointing the corpse. Since it became dark too soon to carry out this project then, they waited until early Sunday morning.

II. EXPOSITORY MEANING. Mary Magdalene is well known as the woman from Magdala (on the sea of Galilee) out of whom Jesus cast seven demons. Mary the mother of James is often identified as the wife of Cleophas, or Alphaeus (variant forms of the same Aramaic original). Salome was the wife of Zebedee and mother of James and John.

"Spices" (v. 1) is *aroma* in the Greek. The "stone" (v. 4) was "very great," probably four or five feet in diameter and round like a millstone. "And Peter" (v. 7) is a beautiful touch, suggesting that the apostle was forgiven, or at least not forgotten, by his Lord whom he had denied. "As he said unto you" (v. 7) refers back to 14:28.

The first reaction of the women was quite naturally one of fear and fright. They fled from the tomb, scared by the angelic presence they had seen there. At first they said nothing to anyone (v. 8). But we know from the other Gospel accounts that soon they recovered their equilibrium and told some of the disciples — specifically Peter and John. Naturally they would not tell outsiders what had happened.

III. DOCTRINAL VALUE. The doctrine of the resurrection bulks much larger in the New Testament than it does in modern preaching. Have we somehow missed its importance today?

IV. PRACTICAL AIM. To see what is the meaning for us of the empty tomb.

V. HOMILETICAL FORM

Theme: "The Message of the Empty Tomb."

Introduction: In the famous Home Moravian Church in Winston-Salem, North Carolina, there is an unusual group of four stained glass windows in the rear of the sanctuary. Looking at them from the inside, one sees on the left of the entrance the scenes of Gethsemane and Calvary. On the right are portrayed the Resurrection and Ascension. By a strange coincidence, which seems a divine Providence, an adjacent building is so located that Gethsemane and Calvary are always dark. On the other side, however, the bright afternoon sun shines through the Resurrection and Ascension. This seems a beautiful parable of the fact that while the lights went out at Calvary they came on again at the empty tomb on Easter morning.

A. *The Mystery of the Empty Tomb.* "He is not here."

It is difficult for us today to put ourselves in the position of these women on that momentous Sunday morning. We have nineteen centuries of Christian history to explain the meaning of Easter. All they had, at first, was an empty sepulcher. There was no Christ there. Not yet had they met Him alive. We have been brought up on the tradition of the risen, living Lord. But to them it was all strange and mysterious.

B. *The Miracle of the Empty Tomb.* "He is risen."

This is the greatest miracle of all history. The Resurrection has been under attack many times in the past. There are still radical liberals who seek to explain it away as a purely subjective experience of the disciples (e.g., Bultmann). But it is gratifying to see how many leading theologians and Biblical scholars of our day are underscoring the fact of the Resurrection as the indispensable foundation of the Christian faith.

C. *The Meaning of the Empty Tomb.* "Go . . . tell."

The New Testament indicates at least three things that the Resurrection means to us today.

1. *An accepted sacrifice.* Paul writes of Christ in Romans 4:25 — "Who was delivered for our offenses, and was raised again for our justification." If Jesus had died but not risen again we would still be left without hope. It was His resurrection which attested the fact that His sacrifice for our sins had been accepted, that His atoning death is valid for us. The Resurrection is the absolutely essential complement to the Crucifixion, without which the latter would not be complete.

2. *An abiding presence.* Because Jesus rose from the dead we may have the living presence of our risen Lord with us all the time. The empty tomb testifies to the absence of a dead corpse. It thereby implies a spiritual Presence.

3. *An appointed judgment.* Before the Areopagus at Athens Paul declared that God has commanded all men to repent, "Because he hath appointed a day, in the which he will judge the world in righteousness by that man whom he hath ordained; whereof he hath given assurance unto all men, in that he hath raised him from the dead." (Acts 17:31). The Resurrection is both a guarantee of our salvation and a warning of the certainty of the judgment.

BIBLIOGRAPHY

Alexander, J. A., *Commentary on the Gospel of Mark,* Grand Rapids: Zondervan Publishing House, 1955 (reprint)

Barclay, William, *The Gospel of Mark,* Philadelphia: Westminster Press

Branscomb, Harvie, *The Gospel of Mark* (The Moffatt New Testament Commentary), New York: Harper & Brothers, 1937

Earle, Ralph, *The Gospel According to Mark* (The Evangelical Commentary on the Bible), Grand Rapids: Zondervan Publishing House, 1957.

Erdman, Charles R., *The Gospel of Mark,* Philadelphia: Westminster Press, 1917

Grant, F. C. and Luccock, H. E., *The Interpreter's Bible,* Vol. 7., New York: Abingdon Press, 1951

Hunter, A. M., *Gospel According to St. Mark* (Torch Bible Commentaries), London: S. C. M. Press, 1948

Lange, J. P., "Mark" in *Commentary on the Holy Scriptures,* Grand Rapids: Zondervan Publishing House

Lenski, R. C. H., *The Interpretation of St. Mark's Gospel,* Columbus: Wartburg Press, 1946

Maclaren, Alex., *Expositions of Holy Scripture: St. Mark,* London: Grand Rapids: Wm. B. Eerdmans Publishing Co., 1944 (reprint)

Morison, James, *A Practical Commentary on the Gospel According to St. Mark,* 6th ed. London: Hodder & Stoughton, 1889

Rawlinson, A. E. J., *Westminster Commentaries,* London: Metheun & Co., 1925

Ryle, J. C., *Expository Thoughts on the Gospels,* 4 vols., Grand Rapids: Zondervan Publishing House (reprint)

Taylor, Vincent, *The Gospel According to St. Mark* (Greek text), London: Macmillan & Co., 1952